The Ultimate Italian Pastries

Virginia Defendorf

COOL HAND COMMUNICATIONS, INC.
Boca Raton, Florida

ISBN: 1-56790-103-4

First Printing

COOL HAND COMMUNICATIONS, INC.
1098 N.W. BOCA RATON BOULEVARD, SUITE 1
BOCA RATON, FL 33432

Printed in the United States of America.

Cover Illustration and book design by Cheryl Nathan.
Author photo by Expressly Portraits.

Defendorf, Virginia
        The ultimate Italian pastries / Virginia Defendorf.
                p. cm.
        Includes index.
        ISBN 1-56790-103-4 : $9.95
        1. Pastry. 2. Desserts. 3. Cookery, Italian. I. Title.
TX773.D297 1994
641.8'65—dc20   94–20104
                                                         CIP

To Todd, Mary, Allyson and Jennifer.
May they inherit their grandmother's
joy of Italian pastries.

Contents

Introduction

After writing many books on the art of baking for classroom use, I knew that the technique of baking Italian pastries could be described in a way that would give confidence to all home bakers as well as professionals.

For more than a decade, I have explored bakery shops all over America. These shops usually feature the old standards and once in a while some imitation Italian pastries. However, since the bakers sometimes do not have the expertise or in-born knowledge of what ingredients Italian people use for their pastries, it is nearly impossible to find the "real McCoy."

My knowledge of Italian pastries was bred in. I come from a background where any kind of entertainment called for these Italian goodies. It is a way of life in any Italian household to have on hand a succulent or creamy pastry. At the drop of a hat, a beautiful table appears for any unexpected guests to savor. At Italian weddings, the pastries are the focal center, sometimes more so than the wedding cake. Every Italian home that I visited and every holiday was a pastry heaven in my growing years. Not only did I acquire the desire to bake these treats for myself, but after years of practice my pastries became culinary delights to friends and acquaintances. It has been my experience that Italian pastries are the people's choice whenever an assortment is served.

For wedding cakes, I started with the basic white batter and lead up to the famous Italian cream cake. My experiments in decorating with marzipan, or almond paste, have won me many awards.

I have addressed groups of aspiring bakers and chefs in the topic of Italian pastries. My confidence has also given me great satisfaction in knowing that the recipes for "the ultimate Italian pastries" (*li ultime pasticcerie Italiani*) will give knowledge to people everywhere and perhaps add to the list of extraordinary bakers. These pastries can compete with French, Polish or Jewish delights, considered by most *chefs de cuisine* as the ultimate. Therefore, in light of the quality, taste and popularity, you can now add the Italian pastries to the honor roll with an added bonus of low sugar and fat for most of these pastries.

Included in the book are snapshots and correspondence from a recent trip my husband and I took to Italy. We spent time visiting some of the local backeries, and to our delight, found many of the pastries included in this book among the delicacies. My husband remarked on numerous occasions that my versions were just as good. I'm sure your attempts will turn out the same way.

When my pastries are served to guests and I hear them exclaim, "Where can we get these?", I feel a sense of great accomplishment and know that you too can serve the ultimate Italian pastries. Serve them often and make different varieties to have on hand. You will enjoy making the recipes and know that you are making the best.

Explanation and Usage of Baking Techniques

EQUIPMENT

There are a few basic pieces of equipment every pastry chef needs to create the recipes contained in this book. Some recipes, such as Rosettes or Cannolis, require special items such as a rosette iron or cannoli tubes. These items are available in most large department stores and speciality shops.

MIXING BOWLS: These usually come in three sizes: small, medium and large. You can find good quality plastic bowls, which lessens the danger of breakage.

DRY MEASURING CUPS: These usually come nested in various sizes from 1/4 to 1 cup. You can find them in plastic or metal, but the only requirement is they should have a flat top to allow you to accurately measure dry ingredients.

LIQUID MEASURING CUPS: These usually come in clear glass with measurements etched or printed on the outside and a spout for pouring liquid. They are available in a variety of sizes from 1 cup to 6 cups.

MEASURING SPOONS: Like the dry measuring cups, these should have a flat top to allow you to accurately measure small amounts. The usual technique is to scoop an ingredient such as flour or baking powder and run a flat-sided knife over the top to remove the excess. These spoons come in plastic and metal, usually in a set from 1/4 teaspoon to 1 tablespoon and work for dry and liquid ingredients.

WOODEN SPOONS: These spoons are excellent for stirring ingredients or using to measure drop cookies. They have an advantage over metal spoons in that they will not break glass containers or scratch non-stick surfaces. However, be sure to clean them thoroughly after each use in hot soapy water.

WHISKS: Whisks are used to beat liquids until frothy and smooth. Professional chefs use a wire whisk to beat egg whites in a copper bowl, but most home cooks prefer to use an electric mixture.

RUBBER SPATULAS: These handy tools are used to scrape the sides of a bowl when mixing or pouring batter into a cake pan. They are also used to fold in ingredients such as beaten egg whites. The gentle rubber will not break down the whites as the other ingredients are being incorporated.

FLEXIBLE METAL SPATULAS: These look like long butter knives without the serrated edge and usually have wooden handles. They are used to spread frosting over cakes and cookies and come in a variety of sizes.

GRATER: This is used to grate citrus rinds by rubbing against the rough surface. Be careful not to get any of the bitter white pith underneath the rind. You can also use a grater for whole spices such as cinnamon and nutmeg.

ZESTER: This looks like a fork with stumpy tines. By running the tool over a lemon, orange or other citrus fruit, you remove the rind without getting any of the bitter white pith underneath.

ROLLING PIN: This item comes in a variety of sizes and materials from plastic to wooden to marble. One of the larger sizes should suffice for most of the recipes in this book. Some types come with a cover and some are hollow to allow you to fill with ice water, which makes rolling easier. Marble rolling pins are naturally cool and are the preferred choice among professional chefs, but the price is usually too costly for most cooks.

PASTRY CLOTH: These are used to roll dough on and to make lifting it easier. They are used especially for pie crusts.

PASTRY BAG: This flexible cone-shaped bag is filled with frosting or whipped cream to decorate foods. It also can be filled with soft dough to form cream puffs or eclairs or other baked treats. A variety of tips are available from fancy star tips to Bismarck tips, which is a long tapered tube that can be inserted into a pastry to fill with cream or pudding.

PASTRY BLENDER: This tool usually has a wooden handle and is used to cut in butter or margarine into dry ingredients. It is often used when making pie crusts or crumb toppings.

BISCUIT CUTTER: These simple tools are similar to cookie cutters but are always circular in shape and have a large diameter. If you don't have one on hand, simply use a round-shaped glass or jar to cut out your biscuits.

KITCHEN TIMER: Most of the recipes have suggested baking times, but ovens vary so make sure you check during the baking process. After a while, you'll get to know your oven and will be able to accurately judge how long something needs to bake.

CANDY/DEEP FAT FRYING THERMOMETER: These are essential when frying or making some of the frostings used in this book.

BAKEWARE: A basic set of bakeware should include baking sheets or jelly roll pans, muffin pans, pie and tart plates, loaf pans, various sizes of round and square baking pans, custard cups, and wire cooling racks.

SAUCEPANS: A 1-quart covered saucepan should suffice for most of the recipes in this book. To melt chocolate or slowly cook frosting, you'll need a double boiler. If you don't have one, simply boil water in a saucepan and place a second saucepan inside, being careful not to spill the hot water.

POT HOLDERS: Do not use a kitchen towel to remove hot pans from the oven. Most are too thin and the heat will seep through to burn your hand. Get good, thick oven mitts and pot holders and always, always be careful when working with hot food.

ELECTRIC MIXER: These come in hand-held models and stand alone models and are essential labor-savers when mixing cake batter and beating egg whites.

BLENDER: A blender can be used to crush vanilla wafers or graham crackers for pastry crusts.

FOOD PROCESSOR: Use the food processor to chop nuts or mix ingredients. Some uses are suggested in the recipes.

MICROWAVE OVEN: Use the microwave to melt butter and margarine.

TECHNIQUES

BREADS: Do not add liquid warmer than 115° to yeast. When baking, tap the crust of the bread with your finger and listen for a hollow sound. This indicates the bread is done. After baking, immediately remove the bread to a wire rack. Allow a quick bread loaf to cool in the pan for about 10 minutes before removing to the wire rack. Tip muffins to one side in the pan to keep them from getting soggy.

CAKES: Place cake pans in the center of the oven to allow even cooking and do not allow cake pans to touch each other while in the oven. To test for doneness, insert a toothpick in the center of the cake—if it comes out clean, the cake is done.

COOKIES: Always allow cookie sheets to cool between batches to prevent them from spreading before baking. Always cool cookies on a wire rack.

PIES: Always cut slits in the top of two-crust pies to keep the crust from getting soggy and to avoid tearing from the steam.

EGGS: To separate eggs, use a knife to crack the egg in the center. Slip the yolk back and forth from one half of the shell to the other a bowl and allow the white to fall into the bowl. Be careful not to let any of the yolk get into the egg white. This will keep the whites from whipping.

INGREDIENTS

FLOUR: There are several kinds of flour used in this book. Most use all-purpose flour which is a combination of hard and soft-wheat flours and is used in all baked goods. Self-rising flour contains added leavening and salt and can be used in quick bread recipes, but do not use the salt, baking powder and baking soda listed in the recipe. Cake flour is made from softer, lighter wheat and is excellent for cakes.

FATS AND OILS: Fats are solid at room temperatures (shortening, butter, margarine), while oils are liquid. Both are necessary in many baked products to make them tender and flavorful. Fats are ideal for baking, but not good for deep frying. Shortening is composed of processed vegetable fats. Lard is rendered pork fat and was once a key ingredient in pastry and biscuits, but is rarely used in today's health-conscious world. Butter is made from milk and contains 80% fat. Margarine is made from vegetable oil and simulates the characteristics of butter. Since it contains less fat, it is a good substitute for butter. Oils are made from vegetable products and are liquid at room temperature. Canola oil contains less saturated fats than regular vegetable oil and is good for deep frying.

SWEETENERS: Granulated sugar is the basic sweetener and is made from processed sugar cane or sugar beets. Powdered sugar (or confectioner's sugar) is granulated sugar crushed to a fine powder. The 10X type is sufficient for the recipes in this book. Brown sugar is granulated sugar before processing. It contains molasses, which gives it color and moistness. Fructose is similar to granulated sugar, but is made from naturally sweet fruit. It can be found in most health food stores. Honey is made by bees from nectar and is sweeter than sugar. Various syrups include corn, maple and molasses. Artificial sweeteners cannot be used in place of regular sugars in baking because the heat breaks down the chemical properties of the sweetener and turns it bitter.

LEAVENINGS: These products cause breads, quick breads and cakes to rise in the oven. Baking soda forms carbon dioxide when mixed with liquid and should be baked immediately. Baking powder is a combination of baking soda and an acidic ingredient which does not rise until heated. Yeast is a plant that produces carbon dioxide from starch or sugar when warm liquid is added. It comes in active dry or compressed form.

DAIRY PRODUCTS: Milk comes in various types determined by the amount of fat it contains. Whole milk has 3.25% fat, skim has less than .5% fat. Low-fat milk has between .5% to 2% fat. Nonfat dry milk is milk with fat and water removed. Evaporated milk comes in cans and has 60% of the water removed. Sweetened condensed milk has 50% of the water removed and sugar added. Buttermilk is the remaining liquid after butter is made. Most buttermilk sold today is skim milk with bacteria added. Yogurt is a creamy dairy product made by fermenting milk. Whipping cream contains 30% to 40% fat and light cream (half and half) contains 10% to 30% fat. Sour cream is a cultured light cream.

EGGS: Most baked products contain eggs. Slightly beaten eggs are whole eggs beaten just to break up the yolk and form streaks of white and yellow. Beaten eggs are whole eggs beaten with a fork or whisk until the whites and yolks are blended and no streaks remain. Well-beaten eggs are whole eggs beaten until they are light in color and texture. "Egg whites beaten to soft beaks" are whites beaten with a mixer until they form peaks with tips that curl over. Stiff peaks are whites beaten with a mixer till they form peaks that stand straight. Sometimes cream of tarter is added to bind the whites together when beating. Egg substitute is permissable in recipes contained in this book.

SPICES: The recipes in this book use a variety of spices as flavoring. Among the dry spices are allspice, anise, cinnamon, cloves, ginger, mace, nutmeg and vanilla powder, which is available in most supermarkets and health food stores. Vanilla also comes as a liquid, either in extract form (more expensive) or flavoring. Other extracts and flavorings used include peppermint, orange and almond extracts. Inexpensive flavorings can be substituted for those on a tight budget.

LIQUORS: Among the alcoholic beverages used in this book are rum, Grand Marnier, galliano liquor, brandy and anisette. Italians sweeten their espresso with the licorice-flavored liquor and use it in their desserts. Most of the alcohol evaporates during baking, but don't worry about those few recipes which it's added after baking, such as Hazelnut Rum Balls. The alcohol content per serving is very small, but if you want, you can substitute a similar flavored extract instead.

COOKING TERMS

BEAT: To mix rapidly with a spoon or electric mixer.

BLEND: To thoroughly combine ingredients until smooth and uniform in texture using a spoon or electric mixer.

BOIL: To cook liquid at 212° where bubbles rise to the surface and break. For a full rolling boil, bubbles form rapidly throughout the mixture.

CARAMELIZE: To melt sugar slowly over low heat until it becomes brown in color.

COOL: To remove from heat and let stand at room temperature.

CREAM: To beat a mixture with a spoon or electric mixer until it becomes soft and smooth. When creaming sugar and shortening, the mixture is beaten until light and fluffy.

CUT-IN: To mix shortening with dry ingredients using a pastry blender.

DOLLOP: To add a scoop or spoonful of cream to garnish.

DOT: To distribute small bits, such as adding butter to pie filling before baking.

DUST: To sprinkle lightly with sugar or flour.

FLUTE: To make small decorations, usually in pie crust, by pressing edges into various shapes.

FOLD: To add ingredients gently to a mixture using a rubber spatula. Turning the bowl frequently, cut down the mixture with the spatula, across the bottom and then over the top.

GARNISH: To decorate the finished pastry, usually with frosting, sugar, etc.

GLAZE: To brush milk or egg on a pastry to give it a glossy appearance when baked.

KNEAD: To work dough with the heels of your hands by pressing and folding. Some electric mixers come with a dough hook to do the work for you.

PEEL: To remove the outer layer of skin from fruit.

PIT: To remove the seeds from fruit.

SCALD: To bring liquid to the boiling point, just until small bubbles form at the edges of the pan. Be careful when scalding milk—if it comes to a boil, it will overflow so be sure to pull the saucepan from the heat the moment small bubbles form.

SIFT: To put dry ingredients through a sifter to combine before adding to wet ingredients. In the past, it was necessary to sift flour before measuring to add air and remove any lumps. Today's flour, however, only needs to be stirred before measuring.

STIR: To mix ingredients with a spoon in a circular motion until well-combined.

TOSS: To mix ingredients by lifting and dropping with a spoon.

WHIP: To beat food rapidly to incorporate air into the mixture to make it light and add volume.

Bread

PASTICCINI CON MANDORLA

COFFEE CRESCENTS WITH ALMOND

Sprinkle powdered sugar over these nutty crescents and serve during a tea or coffee break.

3/4	**cup butter**
3/4	**cup flour**
4	**ounces butter**
1/4	**cup sugar**
1	**tablespoon lemon rind, grated**
2	**eggs**
3 1/2	**cups flour**
1/4	**cup milk, lukewarm**
2	**1-ounce packages rapid rising yeast**
2	**cups almonds, blanched and ground**
1/2	**cup sugar**
1	**lemon rind, grated**
1	**egg white, beaten**
1	**egg, whisked**

In a medium bowl, mix butter and flour together to form a paste. Mold into a square, wrap in waxed paper and refrigerate.

In a large mixer bowl, cream butter and sugar. Add lemon rind and eggs. Continue mixing as you add a part of the flour into mixture. Add milk and sprinkle in yeast. Add remaining flour, kneading it in to make a soft dough. Cover and let rest.

Sprinkle a working surface with flour then roll dough into a long rectangle about 1/2" thick and 10" x 12" long. Spread chilled butter paste on top and fold in half. Roll dough to form a rectangle and fold like an envelope. Cover and chill. Repeat process six more times, each time rolling, folding and chilling. After the last time, divide dough in half, keeping one half chilled and covered. Roll into a large rectangle.

Pre-heat oven to 425°. Combine almonds, sugar and lemon rind. Add egg white and stir into a smooth paste. Spread paste on top of rolled dough. Cut dough into triangles and, starting from long end, roll to form crescent. Repeat with remaining dough until all crescents are formed. Place pastries on a greased baking sheet and brush with beaten egg. Bake crescents at 425° for 10 minutes. Reduce heat to 350° and bake for another 10 minutes or until golden.

Makes 20 crescents.

Dear Don + Janis,

Sicily is everything we dreamed it would be and to our delight we came across the Mount Etna Bakery. I had to keep Ed from eating too many of these wonderful Almond Crescents, but I let him take some back to the hotel. Much love,

Virginia and (a very full) Ed

The Marcelleo Family
4122 Willow St.
Denver, CO 80205

PASTICCI DI MATINA

MORNING PASTRIES

You can use any type of pie filling in these luscious pastries. Try cherry, pineapple or even cream cheese. As a variation, you can mix almond paste with the pie filling. You and your guests will not be disappointed with the result.

1	**cup milk**
1/3	**cup sugar**
1	**scant teaspoon salt**
1/4	**cup margarine**
1	**1-ounce package rapid rising yeast**
1/4	**cup warm water**
2	**eggs**
1/4	**teaspoon nutmeg**
1/2	**teaspoon vanilla extract**
3–4	**cups flour**
1	**cup margarine**
1	**can pie filling**
1	**egg, beaten frothy**
1	**cup powdered sugar**
1	**tablespoon milk**
1	**teaspoon butter, melted**
1/4	**cup walnuts, chopped**

In a medium saucepan, scald milk with sugar, salt and margarine. Cool to lukewarm and set aside.

In a large bowl, sprinkle yeast in warm water, about 110°–115°, and stir to dissolve. Add eggs, nutmeg, vanilla and 1 cup of flour. Add milk mixture and beat with electric beater at medium speed. Stir in enough flour to make a soft dough. Cover and let rise in a warm area until double.

Roll dough to 1/4" thickness on a floured board. Dot with margarine, fold in thirds and roll to 1/4" thickness again. Repeat 5 times. If dough becomes sticky, place in refrigerator 30 minutes then continue. The more the dough is rolled, the more tender the pastries will be.

Pre-heat oven to 375°. Cut dough into 20 to 24 squares. Place 1 tablespoon filling on dough and fold like an envelope. Place pastry on ungreased baking sheet and brush with beaten egg. Sprinkle with chopped nuts and bake at 375° for about 20 minutes or until lightly browned. Remove from sheet to cool.

Combine powdered sugar, milk and margarine. Mix until smooth. Spread on top of cooled pastries.

Makes 20–24 pastries.

PANETTINI
ITALIAN CROISSANTS

These classic rolls are great for serving at brunches or luncheons with butter and a variety of jams, but breakfast always includes croissants in Italy.

2	1-ounce packages rapid rising yeast
1/2	cup warm water
2/3	cup milk
1/4	cup canola oil
3	tablespoons sugar
1	teaspoon salt
2	eggs
3 1/2–4	cups flour
1	cup butter, softened
1	egg white
1	teaspoon water

In a small saucepan scald milk and allow to cool to lukewarm. In a large mixing bowl, dissolve yeast in warm water. Stir in milk, oil, sugar, salt, eggs and 2 cups of flour. Stir in enough of the remaining flour to make dough easy to handle. Turn out onto a floured working area. Knead dough for about 5 minutes or until smooth and elastic. Place in a large greased bowl and rotate to grease all sides of dough. Cover and let rise in a warm area until doubled. Punch down then refrigerate for 1 hour.

Punch down chilled dough again and roll into a 25" x 10" rectangle. Spread with 1/4 of the butter. Fold dough into thirds, making 3 layers. Roll out to same size and spread with another 1/4 of the butter. Repeat 2 more times. Divide dough in half, cover and refrigerate 1 hour. Shape one half of dough at a time, keeping the other in refrigerator until ready to use. Roll dough to form a 12" x 8" rectangle. Cut lengthwise in half, then cut crosswise into 3 squares. Cut each square diagonally into 2 triangles.

Start with wide end and roll each triangle. Place rolls with pointed end underneath and with a slight curve to form a crescent on an ungreased baking sheet. Refrigerate for 30 minutes.

Pre-heat oven to 425°. Beat egg white with 1 teaspoon water and carefully brush rolls. Bake at 425° for 14 to 16 minutes, until light brown.

Makes 18 croissants.

ROTTOLI GRANDI DI CANNELLA

LARGE CINNAMON ROLLS

Make these rolls ahead of time, cover with a paper towel and warm them in the microwave oven. Serve hot as a fancy treat for your afternoon card game.

4	**cups flour**
1	**1-ounce package rapid rising yeast**
1 1/4	**cups nonfat milk**
1/4	**cup sugar**
1/4	**cup sweet butter or margarine**
1/2	**teaspoon salt**
1	**egg**
1/4	**cup sugar**
1	**tablespoon ground cinnamon**
1/3	**cup butter, melted**
1	**cup powdered sugar**
1/3	**teaspoon vanilla extract**
2	**tablespoons milk or cream**

Place flour in a large bowl and add yeast. Heat milk, together with sugar, butter and salt until warm—approximately 120°. Stir to completely melt butter. Add to flour mixture and beat until easy to handle. Turn out onto a floured surface and knead until smooth and elastic. Place dough in a lightly greased bowl, cover and let rise until doubled in size.

Roll dough on a floured surface to a thin rectangle about 10" x 20". Brush with melted butter and sprinkle with cinnamon and sugar. Starting with the short end, roll dough jelly roll fashion. With a sharp knife, cut 2" slices and place on a greased 9" cake pan, cut side up. Drizzle any left over melted butter on top. Cover with a clean towel and let rise until double.

Pre-heat oven to 375°. Bake rolls at 375° for 25 to 30 minutes or until puffed and golden. Allow to cool in pan for 10 to 15 minutes then remove to a wire rack.

Combine powdered sugar, vanilla and milk or cream in a small bowl. Beat until smooth. Drizzle over warm cinnamon rolls and serve.

Makes 6 large rolls.

MUFFELETINA DI PASQUA
EASTER HOT CROSS BUNS

These buns can be topped with chopped fruit and nuts for a traditional Easter treat.

5	cups flour
2	packages quick rising yeast
1/3	cup granulated sugar
1	pinch of salt
1	teaspoon ground cinnamon
1/2	teaspoon ground allspice
1/4	teaspoon ground nutmeg
1 1/4	cups milk
1/4	cup margarine
2	eggs, lightly beaten
1	cup raisins
2–3	tablespoons milk
1 1/2	teaspoons margarine, softened
1	cup powdered sugar
1/4	teaspoon vanilla extract

In medium mixing bowl, combine flour, yeast, sugar, salt, cinnamon, allspice and nutmeg. In a small saucepan, heat milk and margarine to a warm temperature, but do not boil or scald. Stir into flour mixture and beat with an electric mixer on medium speed until well blended. Add eggs and stir in raisins. Knead dough on floured board until soft and elastic. Place dough in a greased bowl, cover with clean towel and let rise until doubled. Divide into 15 equal portions and shape each into a ball. Place each ball on greased jellyroll pan, 1" apart and let rise until doubled.

Pre-heat oven to 350°. Brush buns with melted margarine and bake at 350° for 25 minutes, or until golden brown. Cool on a wire rack.

Combine powdered sugar with milk, softened margarine and vanilla. Drizzle icing in a cross pattern over each bun.

Makes 15 buns.

PANI DI PASQUA

EASTER BREAD

The egg in the center of this traditional Easter bread is a symbol of the fertility of the season.

5–6	**cups flour**
2	**packages fast rising yeast**
2/3	**cup sugar**
1	**pinch of salt**
1/2	**teaspoon lemon zest, grated**
1	**cup milk**
1/3	**cup butter or margarine**
1	**tablespoon lemon juice**
6	**eggs**
3/4	**cup raisins, light or dark**

Combine 2 cups flour, yeast, sugar, salt and lemon zest in large mixing bowl. In a saucepan, heat milk, butter or margarine and lemon juice until very warm. Be careful not to scald or boil! Slowly add liquid to flour mixture. At slow speed, add 4 eggs and blend, then beat at medium speed for about 3 minutes.

Slowly stir in raisins and remaining flour. On a floured surface, knead dough, adding just enough flour so dough is soft and elastic. Place in a greased bowl and cover with a clean towel. Let rise in a warm moist place until doubled. Punch down and divide dough in half. Using hands, roll each half into a large rope and coil inside a greased 8" round cake pan. Cover and let rise until double.

Pre-heat oven to 375°. Carefully remove some dough from the center of each loaf to form a doughnut-like depression and place remaining eggs in center. Bake at 375° for 40 to 45 minutes.

Makes 2 loaves.

PANI DI PASQUA CON BURRO

EASTER BREAD WITH BUTTER

This traditional Easter bread can be sliced and served plain or topped with butter, jam, cream cheese or other choice of spreads.

1	**cup heavy cream**
1	**envelope fast rising yeast**
1/4	**cup warm water**
3 1/2–4	**cups flour**
3	**egg yolks**
1/2	**cup sugar**
1/4	**cup butter**
1	**pinch of salt**
1	**teaspoon cardamom, grated**
1	**teaspoon lemon peel, grated**
1	**teaspoon orange peel, grated**
1/2	**cup golden raisins**
1/2	**cup slivered almonds**
1/2	**cup milk**
1/2	**cup rye flour**

Heat cream in saucepan until warm. Dissolve yeast in warm water in large bowl. Stir in cream and one cup of flour. Blend until smooth. Cover and let rise in warm place until doubled.

Stir batter down and add egg yolks, sugar, butter, salt, cardamom, lemon peel, orange peel, raisins and almonds, beating thoroughly. Stir in milk and rye flour, beating to make a firm dough. Turn dough onto a lightly floured surface and knead, adding flour until dough is soft, smooth and elastic. Place dough in greased bowl and turn to grease top. Cover with a clean towel and let rise until double. Wrap a greased 2" piece of foil around the edge of an empty 3 pound coffee can, extending the foil above the rim. Punch down dough and place in can. Cover with plastic wrap and let rise until dough reaches top of can.

Pre-heat oven to 350°. Bake bread at 350° for 1 hour. Make sure you have enough room in your oven for the can.

After baking, brush top of bread with melted butter. Allow to cool in can about 10 minutes, then remove and cool completely on wire rack.

Makes 1 loaf.

PANNETONNI FRITTO

FRIED PUFF BREAD

These puff pastries originated as a peasant's treat because of the simplicity of the ingredients, but it soon gained the status of culinary acceptance. While they're still hot from the fryer, dust them with powdered sugar and serve with warm maple syrup.

1	**cup milk**
4	**ounces sweet butter**
1 1/3	**cups flour**
4	**eggs**
1	**tablespoon rum or brandy**
	oil for frying

In a medium saucepan, combine milk and butter. When mixture starts to simmer, remove from heat. Add flour. Stir quickly so that flour is incorporated. Add eggs one at a time, stirring vigorously to keep from cooking the eggs. Add rum and continue until dough is glossy and well blended.

Heat oil in a deep fryer to 375°. Drop dough by the tablespoonful and fry until a golden brown, turning continuously. The dough will puff until nearly double in size. Remove with a slotted spoon. Drain on paper towels.

Makes 10 puffs.

PANNETONNE DI MANDORLA

ALMOND STRUDEL

This classic delight is a favorite in Southern Italy and is served for special occasions or simply for an everyday dessert.

2	**cups flour**
¼	**cup sugar**
¼	**pound unsalted butter, melted**
2	**egg yolks**
2	**tablespoons milk**
¼	**teaspoon salt**
1	**1-ounce package rapid rising yeast**
¾	**cup milk**
½	**cup sugar**
3	**cups almonds, ground**
2	**tablespoons unsalted butter, melted**
1	**tablespoon lemon rind, grated**
½	**cup raisins**
½	**cup chocolate chips**
1	**egg white**

In a large mixing bowl, combine flour and sugar then make a well in the center. Add butter, egg yolks, milk and salt. Sprinkle yeast on top then slowly mix ingredients together until dough forms a soft round ball. Knead dough, adding a little flour if necessary. Dough should be smooth and dry, but not sticky. Cover and let rest for 1 hour. When ready, sprinkle working surface with flour and roll dough between wax paper to 1/4" thick. Remove top waxed paper and trim to a rectangle.

In a medium pan, bring milk and sugar to the boiling point, but be careful not to boil. Add almonds, butter, lemon rind, raisins and chocolate chips. Stir and remove from heat. Fold filling a few times to make sure ingredients are well blended.

Spread filling to 1" from edges and roll dough from narrow end to top. Place on a greased baking sheet and brush with egg white. Make several slits with a sharp knife on top of dough and let rise to double.

Pre-heat oven to 350°. Bake strudel at 350° for 35 to 40 minutes. Let cool and slice diagonally. Sprinkle with powdered sugar.

PASTICCINI DI CARAMELLI E NOCE

CARAMEL NUT ROLLS

These rolls are easy to make, but sure to impress your friends and colleagues. Serve them hot with maple syrup.

2	**8-ounce packages refrigerator biscuits**
1/4	**cup butter or margarine, melted**
3/4	**cup brown sugar**
1/2	**cup walnuts, chopped**
1	**teaspoon cinnamon**

Pre-heat oven to 375°. Combine sugar, walnuts and cinnamon. Dip biscuits, first in melted butter, then in sugar mixture. Place in a well greased 9" square pan. Sprinkle cinnamon over top. Bake at 375° for 20 to 25 minutes.

Makes 20 rolls.

PANINI DI LIMONE E MIELE
LEMON AND HONEY BISCUITS

Sprinkle the tops of these appetizing lemon and honey sandwiches with powdered sugar before serving. Your guests will love 'em!

¹/₂	cup butter, softened
3	ounces sugar
2	tablespoons honey
1	egg, lightly beaten
1 ¹/₄	cups flour
¹/₂	teaspoon cinnamon
1	pinch salt
2	tablespoons butter
2	tablespoons honey
1	lemon rind, grated
³/₄	cup powdered sugar
2	teaspoons lemon juice

Pre-heat oven to 375°. In a medium bowl, cream butter with sugar and honey until light and fluffy. Gradually add egg, beating continuously until thoroughly mixed. Sift flour, cinnamon and salt, then add to batter. Divide mixture into 50 round balls. Place each ball on a greased baking sheet 1" apart and flatten with a fork. Bake at 375° for 18 to 20 minutes or until browned. Remove biscuits from baking sheet onto a wire rack to cool.

In a small bowl, cream butter, honey and lemon rind. Add powdered sugar and beat until creamy. Add lemon juice and continue beating until mixture has a smooth and creamy texture.

Spread filling on one biscuit and top with another. Repeat with remaining biscuits.

Makes 25 biscuits.

PANINI DI LIEVITO

BAKING POWDER BISCUITS

These biscuits are perfect for teas. You can serve them with honey, butter or jam.

1 ³/₄	**cups flour**
2 ¹/₂	**teaspoons baking powder**
¹/₃	**cup margarine, softened**
1	**pinch salt**
³/₄	**cup milk**

Pre-heat oven to 450°. In medium bowl, combine flour and baking powder. Cut in margarine with a fork or pastry blender. Stir in enough milk until dough leaves sides of bowl then gather into a ball. Too much milk will make dough too sticky to handle—not enough milk and dough will appear too dry.

On a lightly floured surface, knead dough at least 10 times. Roll out dough to a 1/2" thickness. With a biscuit cutter, cut biscuits and place on an ungreased baking sheet, 1" apart. Bake at 450° for 10 to 12 minutes.

Makes 12 biscuits.

BISCOTTINI DI CAFFE E NOCE
COFFEE AND WALNUT BISCUITS

If you have any extra filling left over, thin with milk and drizzle on top of biscuits before serving.

3	tablespoons butter
1	cup sifted flour
1/4	cup sugar
1/4	cup walnuts, finely ground
1	egg, beaten frothy
2	tablespoons butter
5	tablespoons brown sugar
3	tablespoons milk
1/4	cup powdered sugar

Pre-heat oven to 375°. In a medium bowl, combine butter and flour. With a fork or pastry blender, blend until crumbly. Stir in sugar and walnuts. Add egg and form mixture into a round, firm dough. Knead 10 times.

Roll dough on a lightly floured working area to 1/4" thickness. With a doughnut cutter or round cookie cutter, make 32 rounds, rerolling excess dough. Place rounds on a greased baking sheet, 2" apart and bake at 375° for 15 minutes.

Remove biscuits from oven and place on a wire rack to cool. In a small saucepan, melt butter over low heat. Add brown sugar and milk. Stir until sugar has dissolved. Bring mixture to a boil and cook for 1 minute. Cool and add powdered sugar. Whisk mixture until smooth, adding a bit of milk if filling appears too thick.

Spread filling on one biscuit and sandwich with a second. Repeat until all biscuits are used.

Makes 16 biscuits.

LA DOLCI VITA
SWEET TEA RING

This classic sweet bread makes an elegant addition to your dessert table. Serve with espresso laced with a bit of anisette for a classic Italian treat.

1	**1-ounce package dry rapid rising yeast**
1/4	**cup water**
1/4	**cup milk**
1/4	**cup sugar**
1/8	**teaspoon salt**
1	**egg**
1/4	**cup margarine, softened**
2	**cups flour**
1/2	**cup brown sugar**
2	**teaspoons cinnamon**
1/2	**cup raisins**
2	**cups dried or fresh figs, chopped**
1	**cup chopped walnuts**
2	**tablespoons margarine or butter, softened**
1	**cup powdered sugar**
2	**tablespoons milk**
1	**teaspoon margarine, melted**

In a small saucepan, scald milk and allow to cool completely. Heat water to 105°–110° and dissolve yeast. Add warm milk, sugar, salt and egg. Stir well and add margarine. Add flour and mix thoroughly with spoon. Transfer to a flour sprinkled working area and knead 20 times. If dough is too sticky, add flour. Cover and let rest.

Pre-heat oven to 350°. If using dried figs, soak in hot water then drain. Combine brown sugar, cinnamon, raisins, figs and walnuts in food processor or blender. Blend thoroughly.

Roll dough to a 15" x 9" rectangle on top of a pastry cloth. Spread margarine on dough evenly then spread filling over dough right up to ends. Using the pastry cloth, roll dough from long end and finish with the seam on the bottom. Place on a greased baking sheet and form into a circle.

With a sharp scissor, make a cut 2/3 the way into ring. Repeat around the circle, making cuts 1" apart. Turn the cut ends to the side of ring to form a cartwheel. Cover and let rise in a warm place until doubled. Brush with milk and bake at 375° for 20 to 30 minutes.

In a small bowl, combine powdered sugar, milk and margarine. Mix thoroughly with spoon or hand mixer. Brush glaze on tea ring.

Bread

Dear Jin and Ron:

Oh to be in Rome during Easter Week! Amid the hustle, we found this little bakery near the Vatican. They were busy, but they managed to find time to let us sample their treats. Each year they bake many Easter bread baskets and tea rings with eggs baked right inside! A pastry lover's delight.

Much love,
Virginia

PANI DI LIMONE E SIMENZA POPAVERO

LEMON POPPY SEED LOAF

This attractive cake can be made in a large loaf pan, or smaller loaf pans to give away as gifts during the holidays. The baking time is the same, so have fun!

1 3/4	cups flour
2/3	cup sugar
1	tablespoon lemon peel, shredded
1 1/2	teaspoons baking powder
1	teaspoon poppy seed
1	egg
3/4	cup milk
1/4	cup canola oil
1	tablespoon lemon juice
1	cup powdered sugar
4–5	teaspoons fresh lemon juice

Pre-heat oven to 400°. Combine flour, sugar, lemon peel, baking powder and poppy seeds in a medium bowl. In a large mixing bowl, beat egg, milk, oil and lemon juice. Add flour mixture and fold in with wooden spoon just until mixture has incorporated. Pour into greased loaf pan and bake at 400° for 25 to 30 minutes. Remove loaf from pan and cool on wire rack completely.

Combine powdered sugar and lemon juice. Spoon over cooled loaf.

TORTA DI ARANGI E PROGNA
ORANGE PRUNE NUT LOAF

If you don't have a food processor, finely chop the ingredients and mix by hand. A little extra work will go a long way in pleasing your guests.

1	cup pecans
1	orange, peeled
1/2	cup orange juice
1	cup prunes, pitted and cut in half
2/3	cup sugar
1	egg
1	tablespoon butter, melted
2	cups flour
2 1/2	teaspoons baking powder
1	teaspoon baking soda
1/2	teaspoon salt

Pre-heat oven to 300°. In food processor, add pecans, orange juice and prunes. Process until ingredients are chopped, taking care not to overprocess. Add sugar, egg, butter, flour, baking powder, baking soda and salt to processor and blend well. Spoon mixture into a greased 9" x 5" x 3" loaf pan. Bake at 300° for 60 minutes or until toothpick inserted into center comes out dry. To serve, drizzle with a glaze made from a cup of powdered sugar mixed with a table-spoon of milk.

Makes 1 loaf.

TORTA DI PESCHEA FORMA DI PANI

PEACH LOAF CAKE

For this recipe, use a chocolate that melts well and you'll have good results.

1	**package cake mix, vanilla or lemon**
5–6	**fresh peaches, peeled and sliced evenly**
2	**pounds chocolate**
1/2	**cup poppy seed**
1/2	**cup galiano liqueur**
4	**cups whipped cream**

Prepare cake mix following box directions to make a 9" x 13" cake. Cool completely and cut into 3 strips, making a long loaf. Set aside.

Melt chocolate over a double boiler to spreading consistency. Pour onto waxed paper and create a long strip to cover sides of loaf cake. Sprinkle poppy seed over chocolate and place in refrigerator to harden but still remain pliable.

Place one cake layer on serving tray and sprinkle with liqueur. Spread a layer of whipped cream on cake, followed by a layer of peaches. Place another cake layer on top. Repeat with remaining layers. You may want to secure layers with toothpicks, especially if you will be transporting the cake. Cover sides and top of cake with whipped cream. Trim chocolate to fit sides of cake and hold until chocolate adheres securely. Arrange the remaining peaches on top and decorate edges of cake with a scroll of whipped cream. Place in refrigerator until serving time.

Makes 12 to 15 servings.

PANI DI LEMONI
LEMON QUICK BREAD

This irresistible bread is so easy to make, your guests won't believe you didn't spend hours in the kitchen preparing it.

1	**cup granulated sugar**
1/3	**cup margarine, melted**
1	**tablespoon lemon extract**
2	**eggs**
1 1/2	**cups flour**
1	**teaspoon baking powder**
1	**teaspoon ground cardamom**
1/3	**cup skim milk**
1	**lemon zest, grated**
1/4	**cup chopped toasted almonds**

Pre-heat oven to 350°. In medium mixing bowl, combine sugar, margarine, lemon extract and eggs and cream until light and fluffy. Sift together flour, baking powder and cardamom. Gradually add flour to cream mixture, alternating with milk. Fold in lemon zest and almonds. Pour batter into greased and floured loaf pan. Sprinkle a few tablespoons of sugar on top of loaf and bake at 350° for 60 minutes, or until an inserted toothpick comes out clean. Cool 5 minutes and remove from pan.

Makes 1 loaf.

PANI CON ZUCCHINI D'NOCE

ZUCCHINI NUT BREAD

Serve this hearty bread by itself or spread with cream cheese. Zucchini bread is served for breakfast all over Italy.

3	eggs
2	cups sugar
1	cup canola oil
1 ½	teaspoons cinnamon
½	teaspoon salt
1	teaspoon baking soda
1	teaspoon baking powder
2	cups zucchini, grated
3	cups flour, sifted
1	cup walnuts, chopped

Pre-heat oven to 350°. In a medium bowl, beat eggs until foamy. Add sugar and oil, mixing well. Add cinnamon, salt, baking soda, baking powder, zucchini, flour and walnuts, folding in until all ingredients are fully incorporated. Pour batter into 2 greased and floured 9" x 5" x 3" loaf pans and bake at 350° for 45 to 55 minutes or until a toothpick inserted in center comes out clean. Cool and remove from pans.

Makes 2 loaves.

Cakes

TORTA DI CACIO ITALIANA

ITALIAN CHEESECAKE

This cheesecake is a specialty from the north region of Italy. It's a traditional Easter treat.

3	tablespoons margarine, softened
1/4	cup sugar
2	egg whites
1	tablespoon Grand Marnier
1/2	teaspoon vanilla extract
1 1/2	cups flour
1	teaspoon baking powder
1	pinch salt
1	15-ounce container ricotta or cottage cheese
1	3-ounce package light cream cheese
1/4	cup fructose
1	tablespoon grand marnier
1	teaspoon orange peel, grated
3	egg whites
1	tablespoon milk

In a medium bowl, combine margarine, sugar, egg whites, grand marnier and vanilla. Beat at medium speed until smooth. Add flour, baking powder and salt then form into ball. Cover with plastic wrap and refrigerate.

On a working surface, roll out dough to fit a 9" springform pan. Brush bottom and inside of pan with melted margarine. Trim dough to fit pan, pressing so it clings to sides of pan.

Pre-heat oven to 375°. In a large mixing bowl, combine ricotta, cream cheese, fructose, Grand Mariner, orange peel and egg whites, beating on medium until all ingredients are thoroughly mixed. Pour into prepared pan. Roll out remainder of dough and cut into strips. Place strips on top of batter to form a lattice pattern and press edges together to seal. Brush with milk.

Bake at 375° for 1 1/2 hours or until a knife inserted in center comes out clean. Cool on wire rack and carefully unmold from pan onto serving platter. Serve with a little drizzle of Grand Marnier.

Makes 8–10 servings.

TORTA DI RICOTTA
CHEESECAKE

This Italian variation of the classic cheesecake uses ricotta rather than cream cheese in the filling. If you can't find vanilla powder in the local supermarket or health food store, substitute 1/4 teaspoon vanilla extract and add an additional 1/2 teaspoon flour.

1	**cup graham cracker crumbs**
1/4	**cup finely ground walnuts**
1	**teaspoon sugar**
2	**tablespoons diet margarine, melted**
1	**24-ounce container ricotta cheese**
3/4	**cup sugar**
1/4	**cup melted diet margarine**
2	**tablespoons flour**
3	**egg whites, beaten frothy**
1	**tablespoon orange liqueur**
1/2	**teaspoon vanilla powder**
1/4	**cup orange juice**
1/4	**teaspoon grated orange peel**
1/2	**cup fresh strawberries, halved**
1/2	**cup kiwi fruit, peeled and sliced**
1	**orange, sectioned**
1/3	**cup orange marmalade, heated and strained**

Pre-heat oven to 350°. Combine graham crackers, walnuts, and sugar in a medium bowl. Work in margarine so that crumbs will be evenly moist. Press crumb mixture into the bottom of a 9" springform pan and bake for 10 minutes. Set aside to cool.

In a large mixing bowl, combine flour, egg whites, orange liqueur, vanilla powder, orange juice and orange peel. Mix until smooth. Pour into crust and bake at 350° for 45 minutes. When cool, cover with plastic wrap and place in refrigerator 2 hours or overnight.

Remove cheesecake from refrigerator and release springform sides of pan. Arrange sliced fruit on top of cheesecake and glaze with orange marmalade. Refrigerate for at least an hour.

Variation: The filling can be made in a food processor. Simply add each ingredient one at a time and whiz until smooth.

Makes 12 servings.

TORTA DI RICOTTA CON CHOCOLATI

CHOCOLATE CHEESECAKE

Give this sinfully delicious cheesecake an elegant appearance by topping with whipped cream rosettes. Garnish with slivers of sweet milk chocolate. Your friends and family will beg you for more.

1	**cup almonds, chopped**
3	**tablespoons margarine, melted**
2	**tablespoons sugar**
10	**ounces milk chocolate, coarsely chopped**
2	**tablespoons butter**
1/3	**cup galiano liqueur**
1	**16-ounce container ricotta cheese**
2	**eggs**
1/3	**cup sugar**
1	**cup sour cream**
1/2	**cup whipping cream, beaten stiff**

Pre-heat oven to 350°. Combine almonds, margarine and sugar in a small bowl. Pat contents in a 9" springform pan. Bake for 20 minutes then set aside to cool.

In a double boiler, melt chocolate with butter, stirring constantly. Add liqueur and continue stirring until smooth.

Pre-heat oven to 325°. In a mixing bowl, combine cheese, eggs and sugar. Blend until creamy. Thoroughly mix in sour cream until well blended. Slowly add the melted chocolate, beating constantly on low until mixture has a smooth and creamy texture. Pour mixture into pan and bake at 325° for 45 minutes. Turn off heat and leave in oven for 1 to 2 hours with door slightly open. Remove and cool.

Makes 8 servings.

TORTE CON CACIO DI CREMA
CHEESE CUPCAKES

Kids will love this fun variation of the classic cheesecake.

1	**package chocolate cake mix**
1	**egg**
1	**cup sugar**
1	**dash of salt**
1	**8-ounce package cream cheese, softened**
1	**6-ounce package chocolate chips**
6	**tablespoons butter**
6	**tablespoons milk**
1	**cup of sugar**
1/2	**cup chocolate chips**

Pre-heat oven to 350°. Prepare cake mix according to directions on package. Line muffin or cupcake tins with paper baking cups and fill 1/2 full with batter.

In a small bowl, combine egg, sugar, salt, cream cheese and chips. Blend well. Drop 1 teaspoonful of cheese mixture on top of each cupcake. Bake at 350° for 30 to 40 minutes. Carefully remove from tins and allow to cool before frosting.

Combine butter, milk and sugar. Bring to a boil over low heat. Boil for 1 minute then remove from heat. Add 1/2 cup chocolate chips and beat until smooth or spreading consistancy. Frost cup cakes.

Makes about 12 cupcakes.

TORTA GELLITINA
SPONGE ROLL WITH APRICOT

This variation of the jelly roll is easy to make and will please your guests. To serve, cut roll into slices and sprinkle a bit of powdered sugar on top.

4	egg yolks
1/3	cup sugar
1	lemon rind, grated
4	egg whites, beaten stiff
2/3	cup flour, sifted
1	cup apricot jam

Pre-heat oven to 400°. In a mixing bowl, beat egg yolks with sugar until light and thick. Stir in lemon rind. Fold in beaten egg whites and alternate with flour. Pour batter into a greased 9" x 13" jelly roll pan with a narrow lip and spread to all corners. Bake at 400° for 10 minutes, then reduce to 350° for 5 more minutes, taking care not to overbake. Immediately after baking, remove cake to a sheet of waxed paper dusted with powdered sugar. In a small saucepan, heat apricot jam and spread on hot cake. Roll cake from the narrow end to the top. Arrange on a serving tray to cool.

Variation: Instead of using apricot jam for a filling, combine 1 1/2 cups whipped cream, whipped stiff, 1 to 2 tablespoons powdered sugar, 1/2 teaspoon vanilla extract, 3 teaspoons of your favorite liqueur and 1 to 2 tablespoons of ground, unsalted pistachio nuts. Roll cake with parchment paper immediately after baking. Allow to cool completely before filling.

Makes 8–10 servings.

TORTA DI NOCCIUOLA E CREMA DI RUM
HAZELNUT RUM CREAM ROLL

The hazelnuts and rum in this delicious cake combine to form a sumptuous and extravagant dessert.

4	**eggs, separated**
1/4	**teaspoon salt**
1/4	**cup sugar**
1/3	**cup flour**
1/2	**teaspoon baking powder**
2	**teaspoons vanilla extract**
1/3	**cup hazelnuts, finely ground**
1	**envelope whipped topping mix**
1	**teaspoon rum**
5	**tablespoons powdered sugar**
2	**teaspoons cocoa**
2 1/2	**teaspoons hot water**

Pre-heat oven to 400°. In a medium bowl, beat egg whites and salt until fluffy. Add sugar and beat until stiff peaks form. Sift together flour and baking powder. In a large bowl, beat together egg yolks and vanilla. Fold in the beaten egg whites and alternate with flour and hazelnuts. Blend thoroughly until all ingredients are fully incorporated. Line a 10" x 15" x 1" jelly roll pan with parchment paper and grease. Spread batter evenly in pan. Bake at 400° for 8 to 10 minutes. Lay a sheet of aluminum foil on a wire rack and coat with non-stick vegetable spray. Invert cake onto foil, peel off lining. Cool completely.

Prepare whipped topping mix, per package instructions and stir in rum. Chill.

Transfer cooled cake to a flat surface. Spread with whipped topping. Top with additional hazelnuts if desired. Using the foil, gently roll cake from the long side and place on serving platter, seam down. Refrigerate.

To serve, combine powdered sugar, cocoa and hot water. Drizzle over chilled roll. Sprinkle with additional powdered sugar to make an attractive decoration.

Makes 18 servings.

PASTA SFOGLIATA

ALMOND PUFF COFFEE CAKE

When serving, slice this delicious cake diagonally into wedges. It will be the hit of any party.

1/2	cup butter, softened
1	cup flour
2	tablespoons water
1/2	cup butter
1	cup water
1	teaspoon almond extract
1	cup flour
3	eggs
1 1/2	cups powdered sugar
2	tablespoons margarine
1	teaspoon vanilla extract
1–2	tablespoons warm water
1/4	cup walnuts, chopped

Pre-heat oven to 350°. In a medium bowl, cut butter into flour with a fork or pastry blender. Sprinkle water over pastry and, with a fork, gather into a ball. Divide dough in half. Pat each half into a 12" x 13" rectangle on an ungreased baking sheet. Place each half 3" apart.

In a medium saucepan, bring butter and water to a boil. Remove from heat. Add flour and almond extract, stirring vigorously over low heat until mixture forms a ball. Remove from heat and carefully add eggs one at a time. Beat until smooth. Spread half of mixture on top of each rectangle.

Bake at 350° for 60 minutes or until crisp and brown. The topping will shrink and form a custard-like consistency. Remove from oven and let cool slightly.

Combine powdered sugar, margarine and vanilla. Stir in warm water, 1 tablespoon at a time to desired consistency. Spread over cakes, then sprinkle with walnuts.

Makes 2 coffee cakes.

TORTA DI
CAFFE MARMORIZZATO
MARBLE COFFEE CAKE

This eye-pleasing cake is delicious for brunch. Cut slices into diamond-shaped portions.

1	**cup cake flour**
1 ½	**teaspoons baking powder**
¼	**teaspoon baking soda**
1	**pinch salt**
¾	**cup sugar**
½	**cup light sour cream**
2	**eggs**
2	**tablespoons skim milk**
½	**teaspoon vanilla powder**
6	**tablespoons cocoa**
¼	**teaspoon mace**
½	**cup walnuts, chopped**
¼	**cup fructose**
1	**tablespoon margarine, melted**

Pre-heat oven to 350°. In a small bowl, combine flour, baking powder and soda, salt and sugar. Set aside.

In a large mixing bowl, combine sour cream, eggs, milk and vanilla. Beat until creamy. Add flour mixture and blend thoroughly. Set aside about 1 cup of the batter and pour the rest into an 8" greased and floured cake pan. Add cocoa and mace to reserved batter then beat together with a wooden spoon or wire whisk. Drop batter by the tablespoonful on top of the cake, swirling with a spatula to create the marble effect.

In a small bowl, combine walnuts, fructose, and margarine. Mix thoroughly. Sprinkle topping over coffee cake batter and bake at 350° for 30 to 35 minutes or until a knife inserted in the center comes out clean.

Makes 8 servings.

TORTA DI CREMA AGRO

SOUR CREAM COFFEE CAKE

Sprinkle this tangy and delicious cake with powdered sugar to serve. Your guests won't be able to get enough of it!

¹/₂	**cup margarine**
³/₄	**cup sugar**
1	**teaspoon vanilla extract**
3	**eggs**
¹/₂	**pint sour cream**
2	**cups flour**
1	**teaspoon baking powder**
6	**tablespoons butter**
1	**cup brown sugar**
1	**teaspoon cinnamon**
1	**teaspoon nutmeg**
4	**medium apples, sliced very thin**
1	**cup walnuts, chopped**

Pre-heat oven to 350°. In large mixing bowl, cream margarine, sugar and vanilla. Add eggs one at a time and continue beating until mixture is very creamy. Sift flour and baking powder together and slowly add to the batter, alternating with the sour cream, until all the ingredients are fully incorporated. Set aside.

In a medium bowl, cream butter, brown sugar, cinnamon and nutmeg. Fold in apples and walnuts and mix thoroughly. Pour half of batter in a greased and floured 10" tube cake pan. Sprinkle half of the nut mixture over the batter then cover with remaining batter and nut mixture. Bake at 350° for 50 minutes or until toothpick inserted into center comes out dry. Cool in tube pan upside down until cake starts to loosen, then run knife around edges to release. Cool completely on a wire rack.

Makes 10–12 servings.

TORTA DE CAROTA

CARROT CAKE

This classic cake is wonderful when served for any occassion.

³/₄	**cup flour**
³/₄	**cup whole-wheat pastry flour**
¹/₂	**cup fructose**
2	**teaspoons baking powder**
1	**teaspoon cinnamon**
¹/₂	**teaspoon nutmeg**
1	**egg**
¹/₂	**cup nonfat yogurt**
2	**tablespoons canola oil**
1	**cup grated carrots**

Pre-heat oven to 350°. In a medium bowl, combine flour, whole-wheat flour, fructose, baking powder, cinnamon, nutmeg, egg, yogurt, oil and carrots. Mix thoroughly and pour batter in a greased and lightly floured 8" x 8" pan. Bake at 350° for about 10 minutes or until knife inserted in center comes out dry. Cool completely. To serve, dust with powdered sugar.

Makes 9 servings.

TORTA NATURALE

POUND CAKE

This light, yet easy-to-make pound cake can be served at dessert, or for an afternoon or late night snack.

1	**pound butter**
1	**pound powdered sugar**
6	**eggs**
3	**cups cake flour, sifted**

Pre-heat oven to 325°. In a mixing bowl, cream butter and sugar. Add eggs one at a time. Beat well until creamy. Fold in flour until well incorporated. Grease and flour an angel food cake pan or a loaf pan. Add batter. Bake at 325° for 60 minutes. Cool 10 minutes, then remove from pan. Sprinkle with powdered sugar.

PANDORLA DOLCE
CROWN CAKE

This unique cake takes time, but is relatively easy to make. Serve sprinkled with powdered sugar.

½	**pound butter, melted**
⅔	**cup milk**
1	**1-ounce package dry rapid rising yeast**
2	**tablespoons sugar**
2 ½	**cups sifted flour**
6	**eggs**
1	**cup raisins**
1	**cup almonds, blanched and finely chopped**

Pre-heat oven to 375°. In a large mixing bowl, combine butter, milk, yeast and sugar and set aside until frothy. Beat in flour, alternating with one egg at a time. Dough should resemble pancake batter. Cover with a clean towel and set in warm area of the kitchen for about 6 hours.

Grease a kugehoff or bundt pan. Place raisins and almonds on bottom. Pour batter into pan and let rise until double. Bake at 375° for 30 minutes. When done, ease loaf from pan onto a wire rack and let cool.

TORTA BIANCA

BASIC WHITE CAKE

I've used this basic cake for weddings and other special occasions. Decorate with marzipan and a good buttercream frosting. You can also serve with fruit or ice cream for everyday dessert treats.

2	**cups all purpose flour**
1 ½	**tablespoons low sodium baking powder**
1	**cup fructose**
½	**cup canola oil**
1	**cup skim milk**
1	**teaspoon vanilla extract**
¼	**teaspoon almond extract**
4	**egg whites**
¼	**cup granulated sugar**

Pre-heat oven to 350°. Sift together flour, baking powder and fructose in mixing bowl. Add oil, milk and vanilla and almond extracts. Beat at high speed for 2 minutes or until all lumps smooth out. In a clean bowl, add egg whites and beat until peaks form, then add sugar. Beat at high speed until stiff peaks form. Fold into cake batter, folding over at least 25 times. Pour batter into two 8" round, greased and floured cake pans. Bake at 350° for 25 to 30 minutes. Cool and sprinkle with powdered sugar.

Makes 24 servings.

TORTA PER COMPLIANNO
BIRTHDAY CAKE

This classic cake will make anyone's birthday special.

1/2	cup margarine
1 1/2	cups sugar
2 1/2	cups cake flour
2	teaspoons baking powder
1	teaspoon salt
1	cup milk
1	tablespoon lemon juice
4	egg whites
2	cups sugar
1/3	cup light corn syrup
1/3	cup water
2	egg whites
1	teaspoon vanilla extract
3/4	cup chopped raisins
3/4	cup walnuts, chopped
1/2	cup maraschino cherries, chopped and drained

Pre-heat oven to 350°. In an electric mixer bowl, beat together margarine and sugar until fluffy. Sift the flour, baking powder and salt together. Add to batter, alternating with milk. Add lemon juice and continue beating until well blended. Fold in egg whites until egg whites are no longer visible. Pour into 2 9" round, greased and floured cake pans. Bake at 350° for 25 to 30 minutes or until toothpick inserted into center comes out dry. Cool cakes slightly and transfer to wire rack to cool completely.

In a medium saucepan, combine sugar with corn syrup and water. Stir over low heat until sugar is dissolved. Using a candy thermometer to check temperature, boil the sugar until it reaches 240°.

In a clean bowl, beat egg whites until very stiff. Slowly pour hot syrup in a stream over egg whites, being careful not to cook the eggs. Continue beating on low and then on high until icing holds its shape. Add vanilla and blend well.

In a medium bowl, combine raisins, walnuts, cherries and 1/4 cup icing. Blend well. Spread mixture between layers of birthday cake. Use remaining icing to cover the sides and top of the cake. Decorate and serve.

TORTA BIANCA CON LIMONE
WHITE BUNDT CAKE WITH LEMON SAUCE

You may use other kinds of sauces to substitute for lemon in this recipe: strawberry, raspberry, maple or whatever strikes your fancy all taste great.

2	**cups cake flour**
1 ½	**tablespoons baking powder**
1	**cup fructose**
½	**cup canola oil**
1	**cup skim milk**
1	**teaspoon vanilla powder**
1	**teaspoon almond extract**
1	**teaspoon lemon extract**
4	**egg whites**
¼	**cup sugar**
1	**cup fructose**
2	**tablespoons cornstarch**
2	**cups water**
1	**teaspoon margarine**
2	**tablespoons lemon juice**
2	**tablespoons lemon peel, grated**
2	**tablespoons lemon extract**
3–4	**drops yellow food coloring**

Pre-heat oven to 350°. In an electric mixer bowl, combine flour, baking powder, fructose, oil, milk, vanilla and almond and lemon extracts. Mix at low speed until fully incorporated. Increase speed to high and beat thoroughly. In a separate clean bowl, beat egg whites with 1/4 cup sugar until stiff. Fold into batter, until egg whites are completely incorporated. Pour in a greased and floured bundt pan. Bake at 350° for 30 minutes. Cool and remove onto a tray.

In a medium saucepan, combine fructose, cornstarch, water, margarine, lemon juice, lemon peel and lemon extract. Stir over low heat and bring almost to a boil. Remove from heat and add yellow coloring. Stir until smooth. Cool slightly and serve over white cake.

Makes 12 servings.

TORTA DI LIMONE

LEMON CAKE

Serve this delicious cake with whatever fresh berries are in season.

1	**cup flour**
2	**teaspoons grated lemon peel**
1/2	**teaspoon baking powder**
1/4	**cup margarine, softened**
3/4	**cup sugar**
2	**egg yolks**
1	**tablespoon lemon juice**
1/2	**cup milk**
2	**egg whites**

Pre-heat oven to 350°. Mix flour with lemon peel and baking powder. Set aside.

In an electric mixer, beat margarine, sugar, egg yolks and lemon juice on low speed until fluffy. Add flour mixture and milk alternately. Continue beating after each addition.

In a small bowl, beat egg whites until stiff peaks form. Carefully fold into batter. Pour into an 8" x 8" baking pan. Bake at 350° for 15 to 20 minutes, or until toothpick inserted into center comes out clean. Cool slightly and sprinkle top with sugar and cinnamon.

Serves 9.

TORTA DI SALSA DI MELA

APPLESAUCE CAKE

Place a paper doily on top of this cake and sprinkle with powdered sugar to create an attractive design before serving.

1/2	**cup margarine, softened**
1	**cup sugar**
1	**egg**
1	**cup applesauce**
2	**cups flour, sifted**
1	**teaspoon salt**
1/8	**teaspoon baking soda**
1	**teaspoon baking powder**
1	**teaspoon cinnamon**
1/2	**teaspoon allspice**
1/2	**teaspoon mace**
1/4	**teaspoon ground cloves**
3/4	**cup chopped walnuts**

Pre-heat oven to 350°. In electric mixer bowl, cream together margarine and sugar. Add egg and applesauce. Continue beating until creamy. Sift together flour, salt, baking soda, baking powder, cinnamon, allspice, mace and cloves and add to creamy mixture. Fold in walnuts. Pour in greased 8" square cake pan and bake at 350° for 50 to 60 minutes. Cool. Sprinkle with powdered sugar.

Makes 12–16 servings.

TORTA DI SALSA DI MELA E PIZZETI DI CHOCOLATI

APPLESAUCE CAKE WITH CHOCOLATE CHIPS

Sprinkle this savory cake with powdered sugar just before serving. Your kids will love it!

½	cup margarine
1	cup sugar
1	egg
1	cup applesauce
2	cups flour
1	teaspoon salt
⅛	teaspoon baking soda
1	teaspoon baking powder
1	teaspoon cinnamon
½	teaspoon allspice
½	teaspoon mace
¼	teaspoon ground cloves
¾	cup walnuts, chopped
1	cup chocolate chips

Pre-heat oven to 350°. In a mixing bowl, cream together margarine and sugar. Add egg and continue beating until creamy. In a separate bowl, sift flour, salt, baking soda, baking powder, cinnamon, allspice, mace and cloves. Slowly add to creamy mixture, beating until all ingredients are fully incorporated. Fold in walnuts and chocolate chips. Pour in greased 8" square cake pan and bake at 350° for 50 to 60 minutes. Cool and serve.

Makes 12–16 servings.

TORTA DI CANNELLA E CHOCOLATI

CINNAMON CHOCOLATE CAKE

The mocha frosting combined with the cinnamon and clove spices in the cake, make this dessert very special.

2 ²/₃	**cups sifted flour**
³/₄	**cup cocoa**
1	**pinch salt**
2 ¹/₄	**cups brown sugar**
1	**teaspoon baking soda**
³/₄	**teaspoon cloves**
³/₄	**teaspoon cinnamon**
³/₄	**cup margarine**
2	**eggs**
2	**teaspoons vanilla extract**
1 ¹/₂	**cups buttermilk**
4	**egg whites**
1 ¹/₂	**cups light brown sugar**
¹/₄	**teaspoon cream of tartar**
¹/₂	**cup water**
1	**teaspoons vanilla extract**

Pre-heat oven to 375°. In a medium bowl, sift together flour, cocoa, salt and brown sugar. It is better to whiz ingredients in a food processor because brown sugar is hard to sift. Add baking soda, cloves and cinnamon. Set aside.

In an electric mixer bowl, cream together margarine and eggs. Add vanilla and alternate buttermilk with flour mixture, beating on low until all ingredients have been added. Beat on high for 2 minutes. Pour into a greased and floured 10" x 10" cake pan. Bake at 375° for 30 minutes or until cake pulls away from sides of pan being careful not to overbake. Cool cake completely before frosting.

Beat egg whites until stiff. Set aside. In a medium size saucepan place brown sugar, cream of tartar and water. Stir over medium heat until sugar is dissolved. Cover and let come to a boil. Insert a candy thermometer and let mixture reach 230° Remove from heat and slowly add to beaten egg whites. Continue beating on high, adding the vanilla until mixture holds peaks. Spread on cake. When frosting is dry, cut into 2" squares.

Makes 20–25 servings.

TORTA DI POMO E ACQUAVIATE
BRANDY APPLE CAKE

This delicious bundt cake goes a long way in pleasing your family and friends.

1/3	cup walnuts, chopped
1 1/3	cups sugar
1/2	cup oil
4	egg whites
1/4	cup brandy
2	cups flour
2	teaspoons cinnamon
2	teaspoons baking soda
1/2	teaspoon ground cloves
1/2	teaspoon mace
1/2	cup raisins
4	cups apples, chopped
1/4	cup jam, any kind, for topping

Pre-heat oven to 350°. Spread walnuts on baking sheet and toast 8 to 10 minutes and let cool. In a large bowl, combine sugar, oil, egg whites, brandy, flour, cinnamon, baking soda, cloves, mace, raisins and apples. Using a wooden spoon, fold ingredients together until all are thoroughly mixed. Spoon mixture in a greased bundt pan and bake at 350° for 60 minutes. Cool slightly, then remove cake from pan and place on a wire rack. In a small sauce pan, heat jam with 1 tablespoon brandy until jam liquifies. Drizzle over cooled cake. Slice and serve with additional jam on top.

TORTA DI ZUCCHINO
E CHOCOLATI
Zucchini Chocolate Cake

This recipe makes a splendid holiday cake.

1 1/3	cups sugar
1/2	cup margarine
1/2	cup canola oil
1/2	cup milk
1	teaspoon lemon juice
2	eggs
1	teaspoon vanilla extract
2 1/2	cups flour
6	tablespoons cocoa
1	teaspoon baking soda
1/2	teaspoon cinnamon
1/2	teaspoon baking powder
2	cups zucchini, grated
	Powdered sugar

Pre-heat oven to 325°. In an electric mixer bowl, combine sugar, margarine and canola oil. Mix well, adding milk and lemon juice. Add eggs and vanilla, then beat on low until all ingredients are incorporated. Beat on high until creamy. Sift together flour, baking soda, cinnamon and baking powder then slowly add to batter. Make sure all ingredients are well blended. Mix in zucchini with a wooden spoon. Pour into a greased 13" x 9" baking pan and bake at 325° for 40 minutes, or until a toothpick inserted in the center comes out dry. Cool and sprinkle top with powdered sugar.

Makes 12 servings.

TORTA DI FRUTTI

ITALIAN FRUIT CAKE

You can substitute brandy or bourbon for the Grand Marnier in this luscious Italian version of fruit cake.

2	**cups flour**
2	**cups sugar**
2	**teaspoons baking soda**
2	**teaspoons cinnamon**
1	**cup canola oil**
3	**eggs**
2	**teaspoons vanilla extract**
1 1/3	**cups shredded carrots**
1	**cup chopped walnuts**
1	**cup shredded coconut**
1	**cup candied cherries, cut in half**
3/4	**cup crushed pineapple, drained**
1/4	**cup Grand Marnier**
1	**8-ounce package cream cheese**
2	**teaspoons orange peel, grated**
1	**teaspoon Grand Marnier**
3–4	**tablespoons powdered sugar**
2	**egg whites**

Pre-heat oven to 350°. In a large bowl, combine flour, sugar, baking soda and cinnamon. Add oil, eggs and vanilla. Mix well. Fold in carrots, walnuts, coconut, cherries and pineapple. Line a 9" x 13" cake pan with parchment paper and lightly spray with non-stick vegetable spray. If parchment is not available, simply spray pan and dust with flour. Spoon batter into pan and bake at 350° for 60 minutes. Remove cake onto a rack to cool 10 minutes. Invert and place on a serving tray and allow to cool slightly. With a toothpick, pierce cake evenly and brush top with Grand Marnier, taking care not to oversoak. Let cake soak for at least 1 hour.

In mixing bowl, beat cream cheese, orange peel, Grand Marnier and sugar until creamy. In a small bowl, beat egg whites on high until stiff. Add to cheese mixture and continue beating for 5 minutes, or until glaze reaches spreading consistency. Before serving cake, spread glaze over top and sides of fruit cake. Garnish with any leftover cherries.

Makes 20–25 2" squares.

ZUPPA INGLESE

CUSTARD CAKE

If you'll be transporting this wonderfully delicious cake, you might want to secure the layers with toothpicks to keep it from sliding around.

4	**egg yolks, slightly beaten**
2	**cups milk, scalded**
1/2	**cup sugar**
1/3	**cup flour**
1/4	**teaspoon salt**
1	**teaspoon grated lemon rind**
1/2	**cup rum**
1	**package yellow cake mix**
1/3	**cup orange marmalade**
3	**tablespoons candied fruit**

Combine yolks, milk, sugar, flour, salt, lemon rind and rum in a medium saucepan. Cook over low heat until thickened, stirring constantly. Remove from heat and continue stirring as it cools. Cover and chill.

Prepare cake mix as per package directions, making two 9" layers. Let cool after baking. Place one layer on a serving tray and sprinkle with rum. Spread one-half of cooled custard. Place second layer on top, sprinkle with rum and add rest of custard. Top with candied fruit. Cover and chill before serving.

Makes 8–10 servings.

CHOCOLATI E MENTA DOLCE
CHOCOLATE MINT DESSERT

This chocolate mint delight is wonderful for a mid-afternoon meeting. Slice servings into diamond shapes to create a tasty delicacy.

1	cup flour
1	cup fructose
$1/2$	cup margarine, softened
4	eggs
1 $1/2$	cups chocolate syrup
2	cups powdered sugar
$1/2$	cup margarine, softened
1	tablespoon water
$3/4$	teaspoon mint extract
2–4	drops green food coloring
$1/3$	cup margarine
1	cup chocolate chips

Pre-heat oven to 350°. In a mixing bowl, combine flour, fructose, margarine, eggs and syrup and beat until smooth and slightly thick. Pour into a greased 13" x 9" baking pan. Bake at 350° for 25 to 30 minutes or until cake springs back when lightly touched. Cool completely.

In a small bowl, mix powdered sugar, margarine, water, mint extract and food coloring. Beat until smooth. Spread on cooled cake top.

In a small saucepan, melt margarine and chocolate chips. Remove from heat, cool slightly and pour over cake. Chill before serving.

Makes 10–12 servings.

LA TORTA DI FRAGOLA E CHOCOLATI CREMA

CHOCOLATE AND STRAWBERRY CREAM TORTE

Even though this classic cake is easy to make, your friends and family will be very impressed with the results.

1/2	**cup unsweetened cocoa**
1/3	**cup water, boiling**
2	**tablespoons margarine, softened**
1	**tablespoon vanilla extract**
6	**egg whites**
1/3	**cup cake flour**
1	**envelope gelatin, unflavored**
1/4	**cup cold water**
1/4	**cup milk**
1	**3-ounce package cream cheese**
1/2	**cup sugar**
1	**tablespoon cherry liqueur**
2	**cups fresh strawberries**
4	**ounces chocolate chips**
2–3	**tablespoons milk**

Pre-heat oven to 350°. Grease a 15 1/2" jelly roll pan and line with wax paper. Lightly coat wax paper with vegetable spray. In a small bowl, combine cocoa with boiling water and stir until smooth. Stir in margarine and vanilla, then cool. In a medium mixing bowl, beat egg whites with half the sugar until stiff peaks form. Add cocoa mixture and beat until well mixed. Fold in the remaining sugar and flour. Pour batter into prepared pan and spread evenly. Bake 12 to 15 minutes or until cake is puffed up. After baking, invert cake on a towel and cool completely. Remove wax paper from cake. Cut cake into thirds and trim to fit a 9" x 5" bread pan. Set aside.

In medium saucepan, sprinkle gelatin in cold water. Stir over low heat until gelatin is completely melted. Add milk and heat almost to boiling. In a blender, combine milk and gelatin mixture, cream cheese, sugar, cherry liqueur and strawberries. Blend well. Pour into a bowl and chill 30 minutesor until thick-ened.

Place 1/3 of cake in bread pan and spread with 1/2 of cream filling. Repeat with rest of cake and glaze with chocolate chips melted in a few tablespoons of milk. Garnish with a few extra strawberries.

Serves 8.

TORTA DI NETTARE DI ARANCIA
ORANGE NECTAR CAKE

Add a few drops of food coloring to the coconut to create an attractive and mouth-watering cake.

3/4	cup margarine
1 1/2	cups sugar
3	eggs
2	tablespoons lemon juice
1	orange rind, grated
1/2	cup orange juice
3	cups flour
4	teaspoons baking powder
3/4	teaspoon salt
1/2	cup water
1 1/2	cups sugar
2	egg whites
1/3	cup water
1/2	teaspoon vanilla extract
1	cup coconut, shredded

Pre-heat oven to 375°. In electric mixer bowl, beat together margarine, sugar and eggs until creamy. Add lemon juice, orange rind and orange juice. Blend well. Combine flour, baking powder and salt. Slowly add to batter and alternate with water. Beat on medium until thoroughly blended. Pour into 3 greased and floured 8" round cake pans. Bake at 375° for 20 minutes, or until toothpick inserted in the center comes out clean. Cool completely.

In a double boiler, combine sugar, egg whites and water. Beat with a wire whisk over boiling water 7 minutes or until thick. Remove from heat and stir in vanilla.

Spread icing between layers of cake and generously ice sides and top of cake. Sprinkle with coconut.

TORTA DI CHOCOLATI E CREMA AGRO

CHOCOLATE AND SOUR CREAM CAKE

Serve this delectable cake with a dollop of sour cream on top. Look for the vanilla powder in health food stores or on the spice rack of your local supermarket. If you can't find it, substitute an equal amount of vanilla extract and add an extra teaspoon of flour.

1 3/4	**cups cake flour**
3/4	**cup unsweetened cocoa**
1 1/2	**teaspoons baking powder**
1 3/4	**cups sugar**
2	**cups sour cream**
1	**cup, plus 1 tablespoon butter or margarine, softened**
2	**large eggs**
1	**teaspoon vanilla powder**

Pre-heat oven to 350°. In a large mixing bowl, combine flour, cocoa, baking powder, sugar, sour cream, butter, eggs and vanilla powder. Beat on low to mix thoroughly. Increase speed to high and beat for 3 minutes or until smooth. Pour in a 9" x 13" greased baking pan. Bake at 350° for 40 minutes or until a toothpick inserted into the center comes out clean.

Makes 12 squares.

TORTA CON NOCE DI COCCO
COCONUT CAKE

This classic and elegant cake will amaze your family and guests.

1	cup unsweetened coconut
1 ¼	cups milk
3	cups cake flour
4	teaspoons baking powder
1	cup margarine, soft
2	cups sugar
4	eggs, separated
1	teaspoon vanilla powder
½	teaspoon almond extract
1	cup raspberry or strawberry preserves
1–2	tablespoons rum
1 ½	cups sugar
½	teaspoon cream of tartar
½	cup water
4	egg whites
1	teaspoon vanilla powder
¼	teaspoon almond extract
1	cup coconut, for decoration

Pre-heat oven to 350°. In a small saucepan, heat coconut and milk on low and let simmer for 10 minutes. Strain mixture and press with a wooden spoon to extract all liquid from the coconut. Set aside liquid and discard coconut.

Mix flour and baking powder in a small bowl and set aside. In a mixing bowl, cream margarine with sugar. Add egg yolks and beat until creamy. Add the vanilla and almond extracts. Begin adding the coconut milk to the batter, alternating with the flour mixture. Beat until all ingredients are well mixed. In a clean bowl, beat egg whites until stiff and carefully fold into batter. Divide batter into three 9" greased cake pans. Bake at 350° for 25 to 30 minutes or until toothpick inserted into the center comes out clean. Cool for 10 minutes and place one layer on a serving platter. Place the other layers on wax paper covered platters. Allow to cool completely.

Combine preserves and rum, then set aside. In a medium saucepan, combine, sugar, cream of tartar and water. Bring to a boil. Cook covered for 2 minutes. Uncover and, using a candy thermometer, cook until syrup reaches 240°. Beat egg whites until stiff and slowly add the hot syrup, taking care not to cook the egg whites. Beat first at low speed then at high until stiff peaks form.

Spread preserves between each layer. You may want to use toothpicks to support each layer, especially if you plan on transporting the cake. Spread the frosting over the sides and top of cake and decorate with coconut.

Makes 12–15 servings.

TORTA DI MANDARINI

MANDARIN CAKE

You can decorate this attractive cake with candied fruit, maraschino cherries and mandarin orange slices. Use your imagination to create a wonderful tasty treat for your family and friends.

1   **package yellow cake mix**
1   **3 ½-ounce package instant vanilla pudding**
1   **can mandarin oranges, with juice**
1   **large can crushed pineapple**
1   **8-ounce carton whipped topping**

Pre-heat oven to 350°. Prepare cake mix according to package directions. Divide batter among 3 greased and floured 8" round cake pans. Bake at 350° for 25 minutes, then cool completely.

Prepare pudding according to package directions and refrigerate to chill. In medium bowl, slowly beat pudding, mandarin oranges and pineapple together. Fold in thawed whipped topping. Spread pudding mixture between each layer and completely cover the outside. Decorate and serve cold.

Cookies

PASTICCI DI CROSTATA

CUSTARD BARS

These wonderful custard sandwiches will compliment any dessert table.

½	**cup, plus 2 tablespoons butter, softened**
⅔	**cup sugar**
1	**egg**
1 ½	**cups flour**
4	**teaspoons baking powder**
2	**tablespoons cornstarch**
½	**cup sugar**
1	**cup milk**
4	**ounces butter**

Pre-heat oven to 350°. In a medium bowl, cream butter with sugar until fluffy. Add egg and beat until creamy. Mix flour and baking powder, then add to mixture slowly. Work flour into batter and bring to a soft dough. Divide dough in half and roll each half into a 6" x 12" rectangle. Cut 1 1/2" x 2" bars and place in a greased baking sheet 1" apart. Repeat with the other half of dough. Pierce bars with a fork and bake at 350° for 15 minutes. Transfer to a rack and cool completely.

In a small saucepan, combine cornstarch and sugar with 4 tablespoons of milk. In another saucepan, scald remaining milk, and add to the cornstarch mixture. Whisk until well mixed. Cook over medium heat until thickened, stirring constantly. Set aside and cover until cool.

In a mixing bowl, cream the butter until fluffy. Add the cooled milk mixture and continue beating until texture is smooth and creamy. Spread custard between two bars to form a sandwich. Continue with remaining bars.

Makes 24 bars.

TAVOLETTA DE NUGATOLI E CILIEGIA

DATE AND CRANBERRY BARS

The orange glaze gives these bars a light, citrus flavor that will charm your friends and family. If fresh cherries are in season, you can use them in place of the cranberries.

1	**12-ounce package cranberries**
1	**8-ounce package dates, pitted and chopped**
1	**teaspoon vanilla extract**
2	**cups flour**
2	**cups rolled oats**
1 ½	**cups brown sugar**
½	**teaspoon soda**
⅓	**cup walnuts, chopped**
1	**cup margarine, melted**
2	**cups powdered sugar**
3	**tablespoons orange juice**

Pre-heat oven to 350°. In medium saucepan, combine cranberries, and dates. Cover and cook over low heat for 15 minutes, or until cranberries pop. Stir in vanilla. Set aside.

In a large bowl, combine flour, oats, sugar and soda. Stir in melted margarine until well blended. Pat half the mixture on bottom of ungreased 13" x 9" baking pan. Bake at 350° for 8 to 10 minutes.

Spread cranberry filling over baked oats. Add remaining oats on top and pat evenly. Return to oven and bake for 25 minutes more. Remove from oven and cool completely.

In medium bowl, stir together powdered sugar and orange juice. Drizzle glaze on bars and cut into squares.

Makes 24 bars.

PASTICCINI DI BANANA
BANANA SQUARES

These appetizing squares are best served warm with a dollop of whipped cream. If you make them ahead, warm them in a microwave before serving.

½	**cup margarine**
1	**cup sugar**
2	**eggs**
1	**cup ripe bananas, mashed**
1 ¼	**cups flour**
¾	**teaspoon soda**
½	**teaspoon salt**
1	**cup walnuts, chopped**

Pre-heat oven to 350°. In a medium bowl, cream margarine and sugar. Add eggs and beat well. Mix in mashed bananas. Combine flour, soda, salt and walnuts then add to creamed mixture. Mix until thoroughly blended. Pour onto a greased 9" x 9" square cake pan. Bake at 350° for 30 to 35 minutes. Cool and cut into squares.

Makes 18 squares.

BISCOTTINI CON ROSOLIO E NOCE

RUM AND NUT BARS

The rum in these bars adds a nice zest to these special pastries.

$1/2$	cup, plus 1 tablespoon flour
4	tablespoons butter
$1/4$	cup sugar
$1/4$	cup ground roasted hazelnuts
1	egg, beaten frothy
2	tablespoons rum
$1/2$	cup powdered sugar
2	tablespoons rum

Pre-heat oven to 350°. In a medium bowl, cut in flour and butter until mixture is crumbly. Stir in sugar and hazelnuts, then add egg and rum. Mix well until dough is soft. Spoon dough into a pastry bag fitted with a large star tip and pipe out mound of stars onto a greased baking sheet. Space stars 2" apart. Bake at 350° for 15 to 20 minutes or until light brown.

While bars are baking, make icing by blending powdered sugar and rum.

Remove bars with a spatula onto a serving tray. While bars are still hot, drizzle icing over them and sprinkle with roasted hazelnuts. Cool completely before serving.

Makes 30 bars.

PASTICCINI DI CARNE TRITATA

MINCEMEAT CRUMB BARS

Include these rich bars in your dessert display and you can't lose!

3 1/2	**cups flour**
1	**cup walnuts, finely chopped**
1 1/2	**cups margarine, softened**
1 1/4	**cups powdered sugar**
2	**cups mincemeat**

Pre-heat oven to 375°. In a medium bowl, stir together flour and walnuts and set aside. In a large mixer bowl, beat the margarine and sugar until fluffy. Add the flour and walnut mixture and continue beating until combined. Press two-thirds of mixture on the bottom of an ungreased 9" x 13" baking pan. Spread the mincemeat on top. Stir a tablespoon of flour into the remaining flour mixture and spread on top of mincemeat. Bake at 375° for 25 to 30 minutes. Cool completely and cut into bars.

Makes 47 bars.

FIORENTINI

FLORENTINES

These classic and tasty cookies are a "must have" for any holiday celebration.

5	tablespoons butter
1/3	cup sugar
4	tablespoons corn syrup
1/3	cup almonds, finely chopped
1/3	cup maraschino cherries, chopped
2	tablespoons mixed candied fruit
2	tablespoons raisins
2	tablespoons ground lemon peel
1/4	cup cake flour
12	ounces plain chocolate

Pre-heat oven to 350°. In a medium saucepan, melt the butter with sugar over low heat. Add the syrup and mix until fully incorporated. Be careful not to boil! Remove from heat and cool. Add almonds, cherries, candied fruit, raisins, lemon peel and flour. Mix well with a wooden spoon. Drop batter from a rounded tablespoon onto a parchment-lined baking sheet. Make sure dough is at least 3" apart. Bake at 350° for 10 minutes or until florentines have spread to a 3" round disk and come to a golden brown. Allow cookies to cool slightly and remove with spatula onto a wire rack to cool completely.

Melt chocolate over a double boiler and dip the bottom half of each florentine for decoration. Allow to set before serving.

Makes 15 florentines.

BISCOTTI SICILIANI

SICILIAN BISCUITS

These tasty biscuits can be stored in an airtight container until served for dessert. They are delicious as is, with wine or dunked in espresso or coffee.

2	cups sugar
2	cups walnuts, chopped
2	sticks butter, melted
1/4	cup anise seed
12	drops anise oil
2	tablespoons water
2	teaspoons vanilla extract
6	eggs
5	cups cake flour
2 1/2	teaspoons baking powder

In a medium bowl, combine sugar, walnuts, butter, anise seed, anise oil, water, vanilla and eggs. Blend well. Combine flour with baking powder and stir into mixture. Mix into a round dough. Cover and refrigerate 2 to 3 hours.

Pre-heat oven to 375°. When dough has chilled, divide into 5 portions and shape each into a long loaf about 1/2" high and 2" wide. Place on a greased baking sheet 2" apart and bake 20 minutes. Allow loaves to cool on sheet until easy to handle. Cut loaves diagonally about 1/2" thick. Place cut side down and bake 7 to 10 minutes more. Cool completely before storing.

Makes about 20 biscuits.

Dear Lee + Doug,

Here we are in Taormina,
the Riviera of Sicily,
Italy. Having a biscotto
and cappuccino in front
of this bakery on Via
Emanuel. Everyone sits
outside for pastries and
coffee or cappuccino.
This place is out of a
fairy land — beauty
indescribable. Would
I come again? You
bet! Much love,
    Virginia and Ed.

The Fletcher Family
720 East Heimer
Houston, TX 77076

BISCOTTI DI VINO

WINE DUNKERS

These pastries take their name from the tradition of dunking them in wine before eating.

2	**cups sugar**
1	**cup margarine, melted**
¼	**cup anise seeds**
¼	**cup anisette, or anise extract**
3	**tablespoons whiskey**
6	**eggs**
5 ½	**cups flour**
1	**tablespoon baking powder**
2	**cups almonds or walnuts, coarsely chopped**

Pre-heat oven to 375°. In a medium bowl, mix sugar and margarine. Add anise seed, anisette and whiskey. Add eggs and beat at high speed until well mixed. Mix together flour and baking powder and add to sugar and egg mixture in thirds, beating each time until thoroughly mixed. Stir in nuts. Cover with plastic wrap and refrigerate 2 to 3 hours.

When dough has chilled, divide in half. Shape each half into two flat loaves, 1/2" thick and 2" wide. Place on a greased baking sheet, two to a pan, leaving a space between each. Bake at 375° for 20 minutes. Remove from oven and slice each loaf into 1/2" rectangles. Trim each side and then bake another 10 to 15 minutes until lightly browned. Cool on a wire rack.

Makes 3 dozen dunkers.

AMARRETI DI MANDORLA
ALMOND MACAROONS

These almond-flavored macaroons can be stored in an airtight container until you're ready to serve them.

1/2	**cup roasted almonds, ground**
6	**ounces sugar**
2	**tablespoons cornstarch**
2	**egg whites, beaten frothy**
1 1/4	**teaspoon almond extract**
1/2	**cup blanched almonds, slivered**

Pre-heat oven to 375°. In a medium bowl, mix almonds, sugar and cornstarch. Add egg whites and almond extract and stir into a thick paste.

Spoon mixture into a pastry bag, fitted with a 1/2" round or star tip. Pipe 16 macaroons 2" apart on a parchment-lined baking sheet. Sprinkle with slivered almonds. Bake at 375° for 18 to 20 minutes, or until lightly browned. Cool on tray 10 minutes and carefully peel parchment paper off each macaroon. Transfer to a wire rack and cool completely.

Makes 16 macaroons.

DITI DI CHOCOLATI

CHOCOLATE FINGERS

These scrumptious chocolate fingers will delight the guests at any party. Add your favorite extract to the buttercream filling for a wide variety of flavors.

¹/₂	**cup butter, softened**
¹/₂	**cup powdered sugar**
²/₃	**cup flour**
2	**tablespoons cornstarch**
2	**tablespoons cocoa**
1	**pinch salt**
¹/₂	**cup butter, softened**
²/₃	**cup powdered sugar**

In a medium mixing bowl, cream butter and powdered sugar until fluffy and light. Sift together flour, cornstarch, cocoa and salt, adding to batter gradually, beating at low speed. The batter should be soft and creamy. Spoon batter into a pastry bag fitted with a large star tip and pipe each pastry 3" long onto a parchment-lined baking sheet. Chill in refrigerator 1 hour.

Pre-heat oven to 350°. Bake pastries for 10 to 15 minutes or until slightly dark brown. Remove and cool on wire rack.

In a medium mixing bowl, cream butter and powdered sugar until fluffy and light. Spread buttercream between 2 chocolate fingers to make a sandwich.

Makes about 18 fingers.

FIORENTINI DI SAN GIUSEPPE

BOWKNOT PASTRIES

These pastries are a favorite dessert, especially on St. Joseph's Day, March 19th.

1 ¹/₂	**cups sifted flour**
1 ¹/₄	**teaspoons baking powder**
¹/₄	**teaspoon salt**
1	**tablespoon sugar**
3	**tablespoons margarine**
2	**eggs, slightly beaten**
6	**cups canola oil**

In a medium bowl, combine flour, baking powder, salt and sugar. Cut in margarine. Stir in eggs and form into a ball. Knead on a floured working surface until dough is soft and elastic. Let rest for an hour, refrigerate if your kitchen is warm. Divide dough into 4 parts. Roll each part into a rectangle and cut 8" long strips, 1" wide and 1/8" thick. Make a slot in center of strip and slide one end through to make a knot. Drop in hot oil 3 or 4 at a time, and fry until a golden brown, turning occasionally. Remove with slotted spoon and drain on paper towel. Sprinkle with powdered sugar. Serve hot or cold.

Makes 4 dozen.

CRESCENTI DI NOCE
NUT FILLED HALF MOONS

These cookies can be wrapped in plastic and frozen. When needed, remove from freezer and let defrost, or defrost in the oven at 375° for 5 minutes.

4	**cups flour**
1/2	**pound sweet butter**
1/2	**pound margarine**
1 1/2	**cup milk, scalded and cooled**
1	**package fast rising yeast**
1/2	**tablespoon sugar**
4	**egg yolks, beaten**
2	**teaspoons vanilla extract**
2	**cups walnuts, chopped**
2	**teaspoons honey**
1	**tablespoon brown sugar**
4	**egg whites, beaten**
1	**egg, beaten**
2	**tablespoons water**

With an electric beater, mix together flour, butter and margarine until crumbly. Slowly add milk, yeast and sugar. Continue beating, adding egg yolks one at a time. Mix in vanilla. Blend into a ball and let rest for 30 minutes, covered with plastic. Cut chilled dough into 24 pieces and roll each piece into a square.

Pre-heat oven to 375°. In a medium bowl, combine walnuts, honey and brown sugar and mix thoroughly. Fill each square with 1 tablespoon of filling and fold over to form a half-moon crescent. Seal edges with egg whites. Place on lightly greased baking sheet 2" apart and brush with egg mixed with water to glaze. Bake at 375° for 15 to 20 minutes, or until edges appear lightly brown. Cool and serve.

Makes about 24 cookies.

BISCOTTINI DI MORTELLA

CRANBERRY DROPS

Store these fruity cookies in an airtight container until ready to serve. Your friends and co-workers won't be able to get enough.

1/2	cup butter or margarine, softened
1	cup sugar
3/4	cup brown sugar
1/4	cup milk
2	tablespoons orange juice
1	egg
3	cups flour
1	teaspoon baking powder
1	pinch salt
1/8	teaspoon soda
1	cup walnuts or hazelnuts, chopped
2 1/2	cups cranberries, chopped

Pre-heat oven to 375°. In a large bowl, beat butter, sugar and brown sugar until blended. Add milk, orange juice and egg. Continue beating until ingredients are thoroughly blended. Sift flour with baking powder, salt and soda. Add to mixture and blend well. Fold in nuts and cranberries, turning over until batter is completely incorporated. Drop by teaspoonful on greased baking sheet. Bake at 375° for 10 to 15 minutes. Cool before storing.

Makes 10 dozen.

DOLCE CON BURRO
E NOCE DI COCCO
COCONUT BUTTER BALLS

Your guests won't be able to get enough of these warm, moist treats.

1	**cup margarine, softened**
½	**cup sugar**
2	**teaspoons vanilla extract**
2	**cups cake flour**
1	**pinch salt**
2	**cups pecan halves**
1	**egg white, beaten frothy**
1	**tablespoon water**
¾–1	**cup flaked coconut**

In a medium bowl, cream margarine, sugar and vanilla. Blend thoroughly. Combine flour and salt, then add to mixture. Beat well to make sure all ingredients are well incorporated. Chill for 1 hour.

Pre-heat oven to 350°. With hands, shape a rounded teaspoonful of dough around a pecan, forming a ball. Place on waxed paper and repeat until dough is used.

Beat egg white with water. Dip ball into egg white mixture and then roll in coconut. Place each ball on lightly greased baking sheet and bake at 350° for 15 to 18 minutes.

Makes 5 dozen.

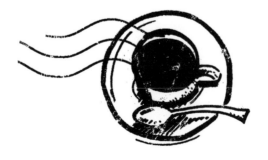

PASTICCINI DI FESTA

HOLIDAY COOKIES

You'll find these cookies in many Italian homes during the holidays. Add sprinkles, chocolate bits, nuts and colored coconut flakes to add festive decorations. The dough for these cookies can be divided and frozen for later use.

3 ½	**cups flour**
1	**teaspoon baking powder**
1	**cup margarine, softened**
1	**8-ounce carton plain yogurt**
2	**cups sugar**
1	**egg**
1	**teaspoon vanilla extract**
¼	**teaspoon almond extract**
1	**teaspoon mace**

Pre-heat oven to 350°. Sift flour and baking powder and set aside. Using an electric mixer, beat together margarine, yogurt, sugar and egg until fluffy. Add the vanilla, almond extract and mace. Gradually add the flour to the mixture and beat until creamy. If dough becomes too stiff for the beater, turn out onto a floured board and knead. Place dough in a plastic bag and chill in refrigerator over night. When ready, roll dough into 1/4" thickness and cut into shapes. Bake at 350° for 15 to 20 minutes or until lightly browned.

Makes 7 dozen.

BISCOTTINI CON PIZZETTI DI CHOCOLATI BIANCO

WHITE CHOCOLATE CHIP COOKIES

These are delightful for school class parties.

1	cup butter, softened
3/4	cup sugar
1/2	cup brown sugar
1	teaspoon vanilla extract
4	egg whites
2 1/4	cups flour
1	teaspoon baking soda
1/4	teaspoon baking powder
1	pinch salt
2	cups white chocolate chips
1	cup walnuts

Pre-heat oven to 375°. In large mixing bowl, cream together butter, sugars and vanilla on low speed. Add egg whites and continue beating. Combine flour, baking soda and baking powder then slowly add to batter until fully incorporated. Increase speed and beat until creamy and smooth. Stir in chips and nuts. Drop dough, by tablespoonful, onto ungreased baking sheet. Bake at 375° for not more than 10 minutes, or until lightly browned. Cool and remove from baking sheet.

Makes 5 dozen cookies.

BISCOTTINI DI ZUCCARO

SUGAR COOKIES

Store these sweet cookies in an airtight container, pop a couple in your child's lunchbox or send along a bunch for the whole class!

1	**cup margarine**
1	**cup sugar**
3	**eggs**
1/2	**cup milk**
1	**teaspoon vanilla extract**
3 1/2	**cups cake flour**
2	**teaspoons baking powder**
1/8	**teaspoon baking soda**

Pre-heat oven to 450°. In a medium bowl, cream margarine and sugar. Add eggs and beat on high. Add milk and vanilla. Mix thoroughly. Combine flour, baking powder and baking soda. Add to batter, mixing until all ingredients are fully incorporated. Cover bowl with a clean towel and chill in refrigerator. Sprinkle your working area with flour and roll dough to 1/2" thickness. Cut cookies with a round cookie cutter and place on lightly greased baking sheet. Sprinkle cookies lightly with sugar. Bake at 450° for not more than 5 to 6 minutes, or until cookies begin to brown. Cool on a wire rack.

Makes about 36 cookies.

BISCOTTINI DI ZENZERO
E UVA PASSA
RAISIN GINGERSNAPS

These tempting cookies can be made in advance and stored in an airtight container until ready to serve. They make a tasty treat any time of the year.

³⁄₄	**cup margarine, softened**
1	**cup sugar**
1	**egg**
2	**tablespoons molasses**
2 ¹⁄₄	**cups flour**
2	**teaspoons baking soda**
1	**pinch salt**
1	**teaspoon ginger**
¹⁄₂	**teaspoon cinnamon**
¹⁄₄	**teaspoon ground cloves**
1 ¹⁄₂	**cups raisins**

In a large bowl, cream margarine with sugar, adding egg and molasses. In another medium bowl, mix flour, baking soda, salt, ginger, cinnamon and cloves. Gradually add to creamed batter, mixing thoroughly. Fold in raisins and chill in refrigerator until ready to bake.

Pre-heat oven to 375°. Using a teaspoon of chilled dough, roll into a ball. Place each ball on a greased cookie sheet 2" apart. Bake at 375° for about 10 minutes.

Makes 2–3 dozen.

PASTICCI DI CILIEGIA E NOCE DI COCCO

CHERRY AND COCONUT COOKIES

These attractive treats will be the hit of any party.

³/₄	cup flour
¹/₂	teaspoon baking powder
¹/₄	teaspoon baking soda
¹/₂	cup sugar
¹/₂	cup rolled oats
¹/₄	cup grated coconut
¹/₂	cup maraschino cherries, quartered
¹/₂	cup canola oil
1	egg, beaten frothy
¹/₄	cup milk
¹/₂	teaspoon vanilla extract

Pre-heat oven to 400°. In a medium bowl, combine flour, baking powder, baking soda, sugar, oats, coconut and cherries. Fold together with a wooden spoon until all ingredients are well mixed. Using the spoon, make a well, then add oil, egg, milk and vanilla. Mix with spoon or electric mixer until mixture forms a soft dough.

Drop dough from a well rounded teaspoon onto a greased cookie sheet 2" apart, leaving room for cookies to spread. Bake at 400° for 8 to 10 minutes or until light brown. Cool slightly and transfer to a wire rack.

Makes 36 cookies.

BISCOTTI DI ANISI
ANISE SEED COOKIES

These cookies are most attractive when you use a special design-embossed rolling pin. Check your local speciality food stores for these unique items.

2	**eggs**
1	**cup sugar**
2 ¼	**cups flour**
½	**cup anise seed**

Pre-heat oven to 325°. In a mixing bowl, add eggs and sugar, then beat at low speed until creamy. Mix in flour and anise seed. Continue to beat until very stiff. If mixture is too stiff for beaters to blend, use hands to knead dough. Refrigerate, covered, from 2 to 3 hours.

On a lightly floured board, roll dough to 1/8" thickness. Press firmly when rolling to cut out designs. Place cookies on an ungreased baking sheet 1/2" apart and let rest for 30 minutes. Bake at 325° for 12 to 15 minutes.

Makes about 6 dozen.

Dear John and Debbie,

Here I am in Palermo, Sicily. In one of the bakeries here, the bakers showed me around. Palermo is the capital of Sicily. Very updated, and everyone so friendly. Yes, I am addressed as Signora here. Everything is so beautiful. Today we view the buildings and mosaics and paintings. So much history, and the pastries are the best in the world. Must return again.

Much love,
Virginia

BISCOTTINI DI MANDORLA
ALMOND COOKIES

You can freeze the dough for these almond flavored cookies, then thaw when ready to bake.

1 ½	**cups flour**
½	**cup almonds, finely ground**
¼	**cup sugar**
¼	**cup light brown sugar**
¼	**teaspoon baking powder**
1	**pinch of mace**
½	**cup margarine, soft**
1	**egg**
2	**teaspoons vanilla extract**

Pre-heat oven to 350°. In a large bowl, mix together flour, almonds, sugars, baking powder and mace. Add margarine and cut in with a fork or pastry cutter until mixture is crumbly. Add egg and vanilla and stir until a ball forms. On a lightly floured working surface, knead dough until smooth. Cover with plastic and place in refrigerator until ready to use.

Roll out dough on floured working surface to 1/4" thick. Cut with cookie cutters and place on greased baking sheet. Bake at 350° for about 15 minutes. If cookies are rolled thinner, reduce baking time. Cool and sprinkle with powdered sugar.

Makes about 5 dozen cookies.

BISCOTTINI CON SIMENZA
SESAME SEED COOKIES

The sesame seeds give these delicious cookies a nice texture. Make them ahead and store in an airtight container before serving.

1	**cup margarine**
3/4	**cup sugar**
3	**egg yolks**
1/2	**teaspoon vanilla extract**
2 1/2	**cups flour**
1	**teaspoon baking powder**
3	**egg whites**
1	**cup sesame seeds**

Pre-heat oven to 375°. In a medium mixing bowl, combine margarine, sugar, egg yolks, vanilla, flour and baking powder and beat until thoroughly blended. In another small bowl, whip egg whites until frothy.

Divide dough in half. Keep one-half covered with plastic to keep from drying out. Cut a walnut-sized piece from dough and shape cookie. Dip cookie in the egg white mixture and roll in sesame seeds. Place on greased baking sheet. Repeat until all the dough is used. Bake cookies at 375° for 15 minutes. Cool on a wire rack.

Makes 36–40 cookies.

LI DOLCI

SNOWBALL COOKIES

These cookies are usually frosted in various pastel colors and served at Italian weddings. Frosting can be made with 2 cups powdered sugar, enough milk to make a paste and food coloring. If too stiff, use more milk. Dip cookies in different colors and let dry on rack.

1	**cup margarine, softened**
1	**teaspoon vanilla extract**
1/8	**teaspoon salt**
1/2	**cup powdered sugar**
2 1/2	**cups flour**
3/4	**cup walnuts, chopped**
1	**cup powdered sugar**

In a mixing bowl, cream margarine, vanilla, salt and powdered sugar. Add flour slowly and mix well. Fold in walnuts. Cover and refrigerate 1 hour.

Pre-heat oven to 400°. Roll dough into teaspoon-sized balls and place on ungreased baking sheet. Bake at 400° for no more than 20 minutes. Remove from oven and cool slightly. While still warm, roll in powdered sugar.

Makes 24 cookies.

BISCOTTINI DI SPEZIE
SPICE COOKIES

Store these savory cookies in a covered container to mellow. They are great sweets for dunking.

3/4	cup sugar
3/4	cup honey
2	eggs
3 1/2	cups flour
1	teaspoon baking powder
1	teaspoon cinnamon
1/8	teaspoon allspice
1	cup almonds, chopped
3/4	cup orange peel, chopped
1/2	cup powdered sugar
1	egg white
1/2	teaspoon lemon juice

Pre-heat oven to 400°. In a medium bowl, thoroughly mix sugar, honey and eggs. Add 2 cups flour, baking powder, cinnamon and allspice. Blend thoroughly until well mixed. Add remaining flour, almonds and orange peel and mix until well combined. The dough will have a hard texture and may have to be kneaded by hand. If dough appears to be too soft, cover with plastic and chill in refrigerator for 30 minutes.

Roll on flowered surface 1/4" thick. Cut with cookie cutter. Place on greased baking sheet 1/2" apart. Combine powdered sugar, egg white and lemon juice. Beat until smooth. Brush on cookies and bake 10 to 12 minutes.

Makes 4 dozen.

BISCOTTINI DI CHOCOLATI VELLUTO

VELVET CHOCOLATE COOKIES

You can freeze the dough for these cookies up to two weeks. Simply thaw and bake for a fresh treat.

1 3/4	cups flour
2	teaspoons baking powder
1	pinch salt
3/4	cup butter, softened
1	cup sugar
8	tablespoons cocoa
1	teaspoon vanilla extract
1	egg
1	cup nuts, finely chopped

Pre-heat oven to 375°. In a small bowl, combine flour, baking powder and salt. Set aside.

In a large mixing bowl, combine butter, sugar, cocoa, vanilla and egg. Mix thoroughly. Add flour and mix until dough forms a ball. Separate dough in half and, using hands, roll each half into a log. Sprinkle nuts onto waxed paper and roll each log to cover each side with nuts. Wrap logs with aluminum foil and secure ends. Refrigerate 2 to 3 hours. To bake, slice cookies 1/4" thick and place on an ungreased baking sheet at 375° for 8 to 10 minutes.

Makes 7 dozen cookies.

BISCOTTI NAPOLITANI
NEAPOLITAN COOKIES

These classic cookies from Naples will astound and please your guests. Sold in packages combining different colors, these appear in Easter baskets all over Italy.

$1/2$	**cup soft butter**
$1/2$	**cup sugar**
1	**egg, beaten frothy**
1	**cup flour**
1	**teaspoon baking powder**
2	**teaspoons cocoa**
2	**teaspoons lemon extract**
2	**teaspoons strawberry extract**
3	**teaspoons powdered sugar**

In an electric mixer bowl, cream butter with sugar until fluffy. Add egg and continue beating until smooth. Sift flour and baking powder together then add to batter. Continue beating until batter is completely incorporated.

In a small bowl, combine cocoa with 1 tablespoon powdered sugar. Add 1/3 of the batter and mix thoroughly. In a second small bowl, combine lemon extract and 1 tablespoon powdered sugar. Add 1/3 of the batter and completely mix, adding a few drops of yellow food coloring. In a third small bowl, combine strawberry extract with remaining powdered sugar and batter and add a few drops of red food coloring. Cover bowls with plastic and refrigerate for 1 hour.

Roll each color dough on a flour-sprinkled working area 1" wide, 1/2" thick, and as long as possible. Cut each strip into 1" pieces and layer each to form a brown, yellow and red cookie. Press to join edges and transfer to a greased cookie sheet. Continue until all dough is used. Chill cookies for 30 minutes before baking.

Pre-heat oven to 400°. Bake at 400° for 10 to 12 minutes. Remove with spatula and cool completely on a wire rack.

Makes 5 dozen cookies.

Dear Jack + Chelle,

On our way to the Vatican, just passed by a pastry shop. Italy is pastry heaven — just like what I make at home.

Saw Pope today saying mass - Went to the Sistine Chapel + Coliseum. Great experience!

See you soon,
Virginia

Classic Italian Desserts

CROSTATA DI FRUTA

ITALIAN FRUIT TART

Top these fresh and tangy tarts with a dollop of whipped cream when ready to serve. Use apples or peaches in the filling or a combination of both to create a delectable dessert dish.

2	**cups flour**
1/3	**cup sugar**
2	**teaspoons baking powder**
3/4	**cup margarine**
1	**egg**
4	**tablespoons milk**
1	**teaspoon vanilla extract**
3–4	**cups fruit, peeled and sliced thin**

Pre-heat oven to 375°. Combine flour, sugar and baking powder in a medium bowl. Add margarine and cut into mixture with a fork or pastry blender until crumbly. Add egg, milk and vanilla. Stir together and gather into a ball. Knead on a floured working surface until smooth. Roll out dough and cut to fit small tart tins. Place rolled dough into tins and trim. Fill each tart with sliced fruit. Arrange strips of rolled dough to form a lattice pattern crust and brush with milk or egg yolk. Sprinkle with sugar and bake at 375° for 45 minutes or until crust is lightly browned. Serve warm.

Makes 8 tarts.

TORTELLA DI FRUTTA
FRUIT CRUNCH PIE

You can use apples, peaches, cherries or rhubarb in this pie. Serve warm with a dollop of whipped cream for a mouth-watering dessert.

5	**cups fruit**
3	**tablespoons sugar**
1	**tablespoon flour**
3/4	**cup quick oats**
3/4	**cup light brown sugar**
1/3	**cup margarine, softened**
1/3	**cup walnuts, coarsely chopped**
2	**tablespoons cornstarch**

Pre-heat oven to 400°. In a large bowl, combine fruit, sugar and flour. Toss well and pour into a 10" deep pie plate and set aside. In a medium bowl, combine oats, brown sugar, margarine, walnuts and cornstarch, cutting in the margarine with a pastry blender or a fork until mixed well. Spoon over fruit. Bake at 400° for 25 to 35 minutes.

Makes 6 servings.

TORTA DI MERENGA BACCA

MERINGUE RASPBERRY PIE

This classic pie is easy to make and is a refreshing treat any time of the year.

1/2	cup sugar, divided
1/4	cup finely ground toasted almonds
2	tablespoons cornstarch
2	egg whites, room temperature
1/8	teaspoon cream of tartar
1	quart vanilla ice cream, softened
4	cups fresh raspberries
1/2	cup sugar
1	tablespoon cornstarch
1/3	cup water
1	pint raspberries

Pre-heat oven to 275°. In a small bowl, combine 1/4 cup sugar, almonds and cornstarch. In another small bowl, beat egg whites until foamy. Add cream of tartar and remaining sugar, beating until stiff peaks form. Carefully fold in almond mixture. Spread meringue evenly on bottom and up sides of a 9" greased pie plate. With remaining meringue, fill a pastry bag and pipe a decorative edge to form a deep shell. Bake at 275° for 1 hour. Turn off heat, leave meringue in oven with door closed for another hour. Remove from oven and cool completely on wire rack. Just before serving, fill meringue with ice cream and top with berries.

In a medium saucepan, combine sugar and cornstarch. Gradually stir in water until smooth. Add raspberries and keep on stirring. Over medium heat bring to a boil and cook for 1 minute, stirring constantly. Pie can be served with warm or cold raspberry sauce.

Makes 8 servings.

TORTA DI CROSTATA

CUSTARD PIE

This tempting pie is delicious when served cold, so it can easily be made ahead of time. For an added touch, serve with a dollop of whipped cream and sprinkle on a bit of cinnamon.

1/2	cup butter or margarine
1/2	teaspoon salt
1 1/2	cups flour
4–6	tablespoons ice water
1	egg white, beaten frothy
3	eggs
1/4	cup sugar
1/4	teaspoon salt
1/8	teaspoon mace
2	cups milk, scalded

Pre-heat oven to 425°. In a medium mixing bowl, combine flour and salt. Cut in margarine until the pieces are the size of small peas. Add ice water and mix until dough forms into a ball. Divide dough in half, and on a floured working area, roll to size of pie plate. Place pastry in pie pan and brush with egg white.

In a mixing bowl, beat eggs and sugar. Add salt and mace and blend well. Slowly stir in hot milk. Pour in prepared pie shell and bake at 425° for 10 minutes. Reduce heat to 350° and continue baking for 30 minutes more or until knife inserted in center comes out clean. Cool and slice into wedges to serve.

Variation: The remaining half of pastry dough can be used to top this pie or stored in the freezer until needed. For a two-crust pie, brush top crust with egg white or milk to give a shiny gloss and cut vents to allow the steam to escape.

Makes 8 servings.

CANNOLI
CREAM ROLLS

These pastries are classically Italian and make an elegant presentation. Essentially easy to make, they are best served immediately after preparation.

2	**cups cake flour**
1/2	**teaspoon baking powder**
3	**tablespoons soft margarine**
1	**teaspoon sugar**
1	**tablespoon lemon juice**
1–2	**tablespoons water**
1	**pound ricotta cheese**
1/4	**cup sugar**
1/2	**teaspoon ground cinnamon**
1/2	**cup chocolate chips**
1/4	**cup walnuts, finely ground**

In medium bowl, combine flour, baking powder, margarine, sugar, lemon juice and water. Mix ingredients until a soft ball forms. Cover dough with plastic and refrigerate for 1 hour or overnight.

Pre-heat oven to 400°. Grease 12 aluminum cannoli forms. Divide dough into 12 equal pieces and roll each piece on floured surface to 7" x 7" square. Place an aluminum form in center of square and trim. Brush edges with water and overlap to seal. Place on a greased baking sheet and bake at 400° for 15 to 20 minutes or until light brown. Remove and cool slightly. To remove aluminum form, hold the pastry with one hand and with a knife handle, gently tap form. It should slide out smoothly.

In a medium bowl, mix cheese, sugar, cinnamon and chocolate chips until well blended. Fill a pastry bag fitted with a large star tip. Squeeze filling into each end of baked pastry until filling is visible from each end. Gently dip ends in finely ground walnuts. Sprinkle powder sugar on top of each roll and serve.

Makes 12 cannoli.

Dear Rose,

While at Taormina in Sicily, the baker of Mt. Etna Bakery and I explored his cannoli. Were they good? Exactly like the ones I make - excellent!

What a place of beauty - One needs 3 months just to see some of Italy. Must return.

See you soon,

Virginia

CROSTATA DOLCE DE CILIEGIA
SWEET CHERRY NUT TART

The combination of fresh cherries and nuts in this delicious tart create an unbelievable culinary delight. If fresh cherries are not in season, simply use a can of cherry pie filling. You can also substitute almonds for the pecans.

¹/₄	**cup sour cream**
1	**egg yolk**
1	**package dry yeast**
2	**tablespoons sugar**
1	**pinch salt**
¹/₄	**teaspoon vanilla powder**
6	**tablespoons margarine, softened**
1 ¹/₄	**cups flour**
1	**cup pecans, chopped and toasted**
¹/₄	**cup sugar**
1	**tablespoon milk**
¹/₂	**teaspoon vanilla powder**
5	**cups dark or light sweet cherries**
1	**cup lemon juice**
¹/₄	**cup sugar**
4	**teaspoons cornstarch**

In a medium bowl, combine sour cream, egg yolk, yeast, sugar, salt and vanilla. Let stand 10 minutes. In a separate bowl, cut margarine into flour until crumbly. Make a well in the center with a wooden spoon and slowly add the yeast mixture. Stir thoroughly. Wrap dough in plastic and chill 1 to 2 hours.

Pre-heat oven to 350°. Roll or press dough into a 9" springform pan and bake at 350° for 15 minutes.

Combine pecans, sugar, milk and vanilla powder and spoon mixture over baked crust. Bake an additional 20 minutes until crust is golden brown. Set aside to cool.

Stem and pit cherries, then dip in lemon juice to retain color. Place in medium saucepan and add sugar. Let stand for a few minutes until juices seep out of cherries. If there's not enough juice, add a little apple or orange juice to equal 1/2 cup. Stir in cornstarch and cook until thickened, stirring constantly. Spoon cherry mixture over nut filling and chill. To serve, remove the sides of the springform pan and carefully place tart on serving tray. Sprinkle with powdered sugar.

Makes 8 servings.

PASTA DI CREMA

ECLAIRS

Your guests will have a hard time believing you made these classic pastries yourself.

6	**tablespoons margarine, softened**
3/4	**cup water**
3/4	**cup all purpose flour**
3	**eggs or 4 egg whites**
2	**3 1/2-ounce packages lemon pudding mix**
2	**squares unsweetened chocolate**
2	**tablespoons margarine**
1 1/2	**cups powdered sugar**
3	**tablespoons lowfat milk**

Pre-heat oven to 425°. In a medium saucepan, bring margarine and water to a boil. Reduce heat to medium-low and stir in flour. Cook until mixture forms a ball, stirring constantly. Remove from heat. Add eggs one at a time, beating thoroughly until dough is smooth. Be careful not to cook the eggs. Spoon dough onto an ungreased baking sheet, forming strips 5" long and 1" thick. Bake at 425° for 20 minutes, then reduce heat to 350° and bake 30 minutes more. Cool completely.

Prepare pudding according to package directions, but reduce liquid by 1/2 cup. Cool covered with wax paper.

Fill pastries with pudding using a pastry bag fitted with a long nozzle or, if bag is not available, cut pastries in half and spoon pudding in center. Fill pastries generously with pudding.

Melt chocolate and margarine over medium heat using a double boiler. Remove from heat and stir in powdered sugar and milk to spreading consistency. Spread glaze on top of eclairs.

Makes 6–10 eclairs.

PASTICCI DI CREMA

CREAM FILLED PASTRY

Serve these delicious pastries on a lacy doily for a lovely accent to your party buffet.

1	**cup butter**
1/2	**cup sour cream**
1 1/2	**cups flour**
1	**3-ounce package instant vanilla pudding**
1	**cup milk**
1	**cup powdered sugar**
2	**tablespoons milk**
1	**teaspoon butter, melted**
3	**tablespoons cocoa, optional**

Pre-heat oven to 375°. Cut butter into flour until crumbly. Stir in sour cream until completely blended and mixture has formed a ball. Divide dough in half. Cover with plastic and refrigerate overnight, or at least 8 hours. When ready, roll half the dough into a 12" x 10" inch rectangle. Cut each rectangle into three, 4" strips. Brush each with 1 tablespoon water mixed with 3 tablespoons sugar. Place on ungreased baking tray and cut each strip into 2" pieces, ending so that each pastry measures 2" x 4". Repeat with other half. Bake both halves in 375° oven for 15 to 18 minutes or until pastries are lightly brown and crisp. Remove and cool. Set aside.

In a medium bowl using electric beater on high, beat pudding with milk until thick enough to spread. Chill until ready to fill pastries.

Place 10 pastries on a tray. Spread pudding on each and top with another pastry. Spread a second layer of pudding then top with a final pastry.

In a small bowl, combine powdered sugar, milk, butter and cocoa, if desired. Mix thoroughly. Spread glaze on top of pastries.

Makes 10 pastries.

BIGNOLA DI CREMA

CREAM PUFFS

These classic pastries are always a tasty treat for any special occasion. They're most attractive when served on a lacy doily.

3/4	**cup water**
1/4	**cup milk**
1/4	**teaspoon salt**
1	**stick unsalted butter or margarine**
1 1/4	**cups flour**
4	**large eggs**
1	**tablespoon milk blended with 1 egg**
1	**8-ounce package instant vanilla pudding**

Pre-heat oven to 425°. In a medium sauce pan, combine water, milk, salt and butter. Bring to a rolling boil over medium-high heat and add flour all at once. Stir until paste pulls away from sides of pan. Continue cooking for 2 minutes, stirring constantly. Remove from heat and cool slightly.

Add eggs one at a time, beating until paste turns shiny before adding the next egg. The paste must retain its consistency of thickness when spooned onto a baking sheet.

Line a baking sheet with parchment paper. Spoon or pipe the paste mixture with a pastry bag onto the prepared sheet in mounds. Lightly brush each pastry with milk and egg mixture. Bake at 425° for 15 minutes, then reduce heat to 375° and bake an additional 10 minutes. Turn heat off and leave puffs in oven about 30 minutes. Lightly prick puffs with a fork to let steam escape. Allow puffs to cool completely before filling.

Prepare pudding according to directions on box and add a 1 pinch of cinnamon and a 1 pinch of mace. Refrigerate until ready to fill puffs.

Cut each puff in half and spoon pudding mixture onto bottom half of puff. Top with remaining half. If you have a Bismarck filler—a long nozzle attached to pastry bag—fill the bag with the pudding mixture and fill each puff. Drizzle cream puffs with chocolate syrup, if desired, or sprinkle with powdered sugar.

Makes 12 cream puffs.

MERINGA DI NOCCIUOLA

HAZELNUT MERINGUES

These wonderful meringue pastries can be made ahead and stored in an airtight container.

³/₄	**cup hazelnuts, ground**
1	**tablespoon cornstarch**
2	**tablespoons sugar**
6	**egg whites**
³/₄	**cup sugar**
2	**cups whipped cream or whipped topping**
¹/₂	**cup hazelnuts, chopped**

Pre-heat oven to 275°. In a medium bowl, combine hazelnuts, cornstarch and sugar, rubbing with hands until nuts are thoroughly coated.

In a medium mixing bowl, combine egg whites and sugar. Beat on low speed. When eggs turn frothy, increase speed to high and beat until stiff peaks form. Fold the nuts into the egg whites, turning to make sure ingredients are entirely incorporated. Spoon in a pastry bag with a 1/2" round tip and squeeze out 12 spiral circles about 2" in diameter on a parchment-lined baking sheet. Bake at 275° for 1 hour or until firm. Remove to wire rack to cool.

Spoon whipped cream into pastry bag with half inch star tip. Squeeze a small mound on top of each meringue. Sprinkle with chopped hazelnuts and powdered sugar.

Makes 12 pastries.

Dear Mary,

We're in Rome at the Treve Fountain. Guess where I am — in the bakery!

These are meringues, Large meringues. I threw a coin in the fountain so I won't miss returning to Rome. Much love,

Virginia

Mary Deffenday
24112 Wilton Road
Oakland, CA 94611

SFINGEE

CINNAMON PUFFS

Place these tasty treats on a serving tray and sprinkle with powdered sugar to serve.

2	**eggs**
1/4	**cup fructose**
1/2	**cup ricotta cheese, or cottage cheese**
1 1/2	**cups flour**
2	**teaspoons baking powder**
1/8	**teaspoon cinnamon**
1/2	**cup skim milk**
6	**cups canola oil**

In a medium bowl, beat eggs and fructose. Add ricotta cheese and blend thoroughly. Add flour, baking powder, cinnamon and milk. Blend until smooth and completely mixed.

In a deep fryer, heat about 6 cups canola oil to 375°. Carefully drop spoonfuls of the batter into the hot oil and keep turning with a slotted spoon. Fry until puffs are golden on all sides. Remove with slotted spoon and drain on paper towels.

Makes 25–30 puffs.

BISCOTTINI DI MERINGA

MERINGUE SWIRLS

These cookies are piled high in the pastry shops of Italy. They are excellent served with cappuchino.

2	**egg whites**
1/2	**teaspoon vanilla powder**
1/4	**teaspoon cream of tartar**
1/2	**cup sugar**

Pre-heat oven to 300°. Line a baking sheet with parchment paper and set aside. In a medium bowl, beat egg whites with vanilla and cream of tartar on high until slightly stiff. Add sugar and beat until stiff and glossy—peaks will stand up. Spoon mixture in a pastry bag fitted 1/2" star tip. If tip is not available, cut end to form 1/2" opening. Squeeze out swirly mounds about 1 1/2" high, 2" apart on lined baking sheet. Lightly sprinkle with nuts, sprinkles, seeds, and so on. Bake at 300° for 30 minutes. Turn off oven and leave swirls in oven with door closed one hour. Store in an airtight container.

Makes about 36 swirls.

CUCIDATI DI NATALI

CHRISTMAS FIG PASTRIES

You can serve these tasty fig pastries just as they are, or with a light glaze of powdered sugar mixed with a few drops of milk.

3 ½	**cups all purpose flour**
1	**cup granulated sugar**
2 ½	**teaspoons baking powder**
1	**large egg**
¼	**cup skim milk**
1	**teaspoon vanilla extract**
1	**teaspoon almond extract**
1	**pound dried figs**
½	**cup raisins**
2	**cups walnuts, chopped**
1	**12-ounce package chocolate chips**
1	**teaspoon orange peel, grated**
½	**cup honey or corn syrup**
¼	**cup orange juice**
¼	**cup brandy**
1	**egg yolk**

Pre-heat oven to 350°. Combine flour, sugar and baking powder in a large mixing bowl. Add egg, milk, and the vanilla and almond extracts. Using an electric mixer, beat until dough leaves sides of bowl. Turn dough out onto a floured table top and knead by hand until soft. Try not to handle dough any more than necessary. Return dough to bowl and cover. Let rest in the refrigerator until ready to fill.

The filling for this dough is best made in a food processor. If you don't have one, simply finely chop the figs, walnuts, chocolate chips and raisins.

In a medium saucepan, boil water, then add figs and raisins. Reduce heat and let simmer for 10 minutes. Strain.

In a food processor, combine figs, raisins, walnuts, chocolate chips and orange peel. Add honey or corn syrup, orange juice and brandy. Blend thoroughly and set aside.

Remove dough from refrigerator and cut small pieces at a time. Roll each piece into a 5" x 5" square. Place a tablespoon of the fig mixture in center. Moisten edges with water and shape into quarter moon crescents. Press the ends with a fork or use a crimper tool. Place each pastry on a lightly greased baking sheet and brush with egg yolk. Make a small cut into the center of each pastry with a knife using a design of your choice. Bake at 350° for 25 minutes or until lightly browned.

Makes 36 pastries.

LA CASA DE LI PASTICCIOLI
PASTRY HOUSE

This house might take some practice to perfect, but when you do, your family will be astounded with the results. Use your imagination to create different designs.

1	**cup sugar**
1/2	**cup water**
1/2	**cup dark corn syrup**
1/2	**teaspoon ground ginger**
1	**teaspoon cinnamon**
1/2	**teaspoon black pepper**
1	**cup margarine, softened**
4	**cups flour**
2	**teaspoons baking powder**
3	**egg whites**
4	**cups powdered sugar**
1/2	**teaspoon cream of tartar**
1	**teaspoon lemon juice**
	Shredded wheat
	Breadsticks
	Gumdrops

In a small saucepan, bring sugar, water, syrup, ginger, cinnamon and black pepper to a boil. Remove from heat and set aside.

Place margarine in a large bowl and slowly add hot syrup, stirring until margarine melts. Cool slightly. Stir in flour and baking powder then mix until well blended. Refrigerate up to 2 hours, while you cut out a cardboard pattern of a house making a roof, four sides, chimney, door, windows and any other ideas that come to mind.

Pre-heat oven to 475°. Divide dough into 4 equal portions. Roll out dough on a floured working area to 1/4" thick. Lay the patterns over the dough and cut with a sharp knife. Use a spatula to carefully transfer the dough to a lightly greased baking sheet.

Bake at 475° for 15 minutes, being careful not to scorch ends. Remove carefully with a spatula and place on a flat surface to cool.

In a medium bowl, combine egg whites, sugar, cream of tartar and lemon juice until very stiff. To prevent from drying out, keep icing covered with a damp cloth as you work.

Assemble house using icing for glue and toothpicks or ice cream sticks for support. Let icing dry thoroughly before proceeding to next piece. When roof, chimney, walls, doors and windows of the house have been put together and dried, add shredded wheat for roof shingles, with icing and breadsticks for the side logs, allowing each addition to dry.

Finally, add gumdrops to create a colorful effect.

RAVIOLI DI CILIEGIA

CHERRY RAVIOLI

Sprinkle these appetizing pastries with powdered sugar while still hot and serve warm. Your friends won't be able to get enough of them!

7–8	cups flour, sifted
1	tablespoon salt
6	egg yolks
1 ½	cups milk
1	tablespoon butter, melted
1	can cherry pie filling

In a large bowl, combine flour and salt. Make a well with a wooden spoon and add egg yolks, milk and butter. Mix dough until a ball forms. If dough is still crumbly, add milk until it becomes easy to handle. Knead dough 10 minutes, cover and let rest.

Divide dough into 4 equal portions. Roll pieces into 4" x 4" squares and cut circles with a round cookie or doughnut cutter. Place a teaspoon of cherry filling in center and cover with another rolled piece of dough. Seal edges with milk or egg.

Heat oil in a deep fryer to 375° and carefully drop raviolis in, a few at a time. Fry until a golden brown. Sprinkle with powdered sugar.

Variation: Substitute peaches for the cherry filling to make Ravioli Dolci con Pesci or pineapple for Ravioli d' Ananasso.

Makes 24 ravioli.

CASSATELLI DI GARBANZO

CHICK PEAS TURNOVERS

These unique pastries are special in the south of Italy. Chick peas are also known as garbanzo beans and can be found in most neighborhood supermarkets.

2	cups flour
1	teaspoon baking powder
6	tablespoons sugar
½	teaspoon nutmeg
½	teaspoon mace
4	tablespoons stick margarine
1	egg, beaten frothy
¼	cup milk
1	16-ounce can chick peas
2–3	tablespoons sugar, according to taste
½	cup almonds, chopped
½–1	cup chocolate chips, optional
	Milk
1	egg white, beaten
	Cinnamon

Pre-heat oven to 375°. Sift together flour, baking powder, sugar, nutmeg and mace. Knead in margarine and egg. If the dough appears too dry, add the milk a little at a time until a soft ball forms. Wrap the dough in plastic wrap and let rest while you prepare the filling.

Variation: You can save time and energy if you have a food processor. Simply add the ingredients in the order given, except for the milk. Whiz once and test the dough for softness. If the dough appears too dry, just add a little milk until a soft ball forms. Be careful not to overprocess.

In a medium bowl, add garbanzo beans and mash with fork. Add sugar, almonds and chocolate chips and mix well. Add milk to the mixture until it is smooth and easy to handle. Do not use a blender or food processor in this step because it will puree the chick peas.

To form turnovers, cut small pieces of the dough and roll into 7" squares (Hint: Trim the sides with a knife). Place a heaping tablespoonful of the filling in the middle of the square. Fold the square diagonally and brush the edges with egg white to seal. Repeat until all the dough is used. Place each turnover on a greased baking sheet, brush tops with any remaining egg white and bake at 375° for 30 minutes or until light brown.

Remove baked turnovers and let cool on a rack. To serve, sprinkle with cinnamon mixed with sugar.

Makes 12 turnovers.

PASTICCINI DI POMO FRITTO

FRIED APPLE PASTRIES

These unique pastries can be sprinkled with cinnamon and served warm as an after-dinner dessert or late-night snack.

2	**cups cooked apples, cubed**
3/4	**cup sugar**
1/4	**teaspoon cinnamon**
1 1/3	**cups flour**
2	**teaspoons baking powder**
1	**teaspoon salt**
6	**tablespoons margarine**
1	**egg, slightly beaten**
1/2	**cup milk**
	oil for frying

To make filling, combine apples, sugar and cinnamon in a medium bowl and set aside.

In a large mixing bowl, combine flour, baking powder and salt. Cut in margarine until crumbly. Adding egg and milk, stir to bring dough into a ball. If dough appears too dry, add more milk until smooth. Knead dough until easy to handle. Cut dough in half and roll to a 1/8" thick rectangle. Cut dough with a doughnut or large round cookie cutter. Brush dough circles with water and place a tablespoon of filling on each. Roll another rectangle with remaining half of dough and carefully place over filled circles. Using a crimping tool or knife, seal edges and remove any excess dough. Heat oil in a deep fryer to 375°. Carefully drop pies into hot oil, one or two at a time. Fry until golden. Remove from oil with slotted spoon and drain on paper towels. Sprinkle with cinnamon and serve.

Makes 8 servings.

SFINGI DI RUM E BANANA
BANANA RUM FRITTERS

These fritters can be sprinkled with powdered sugar and served at room temperature, but are best when they're still piping hot and drizzled with warm maple syrup.

1	cup flour
1	teaspoon sugar
2	tablespoons melted butter
4	tablespoons beer
1/4	cup water
1	tablespoon brandy
1	egg white, beaten stiff
8	ripe bananas, peeled and mashed
1/2	cup dark rum
6	cups vegetable oil

Mix the flour and sugar in a large bowl and make a well using a spoon. Combine butter, beer and water and slowly pour into the well. Mix until smooth, then add the brandy. Slowly fold in egg white, mashed bananas and rum, taking care not to break down the egg white. The batter should be lumpy.

In a deep fryer, heat to 375°. Carefully drop spoonfuls of batter into the hot oil, turning once to brown each side. Lift the cooked fritters with a slotted spoon and drain on paper towels. Arrange on a serving plate and serve.

Makes about 20 fritters.

DOLCE DI NUZIALE
CHOCOLATE RUM BALLS

These rum balls can be made ahead of time for any occasion, but especially for a wedding. Store them in freezer between sheets of waxed paper.

1	**cup walnuts, chopped**
1/2	**pound vanilla wafers, crushed**
2	**tablespoons cocoa**
1/2	**cup corn syrup**
1/4	**cup rum**
1	**cup powdered sugar**

In medium bowl, combine walnuts, wafers, cocoa, corn syrup and rum. Blend thoroughly or process in a food processor just until ingredients form dough. With damp hands, break off pieces of dough and roll into 1" balls. Roll each ball in powdered sugar. Store in air tight container to age for at least 2 days.

Makes 4 dozen.

SAVIARDI DI CHOCOLATI

CHOCOLATE MADELEINS

These classic pastries will certainly impress your family and friends at any occasion.

5	ounces semi-sweet chocolate
3	tablespoons skim milk
1	cup sugar
2	tablespoons unsalted butter
3	eggs
1 1/2	cups brewed coffee, chilled
1/2	cup madeira wine
1	cup cake flour
1	cup unbleached flour
2	teaspoons baking soda

Pre-heat oven to 350°. Melt chocolate in a double boiler with milk over low heat while stirring with a wooden spoon. Set aside to cool.

In a medium bowl, cream sugar with butter until fluffy. Add eggs one at a time and continue beating on low while blending in chocolate mixture.

Combine coffee and wine. In a medium bowl, sift together flours with baking soda. Starting with the coffee mixture, add to chocolate and alternate with the flour. Blend well until batter is thoroughly incorporated.

Spray madelein tins with vegetable spray and fill with batter to the top. Bake at 350° for 8 to 10 minutes or until center springs back. Remove to rack to cool and dust top with powdered sugar.

Makes 40 pastries.

BOMBONE

BONBONS

These light and tasty sandwiches are a special treat your guests will appreciate.

¾   **cup cake flour**
2   **tablespoons cocoa**
5   **tablespoons margarine**
4   **tablespoons sugar**
2   **tablespoons light corn syrup**
1   **egg, beaten**

4   **tablespoons butter**
¾   **cup powdered sugar**
2   **ounces baking chocolate**
1   **teaspoon vanilla extract**

Pre-heat oven to 350°. In a medium bowl, mix flour and cocoa. Add margarine and cut in until mixture is crumbly. Stir in sugar, syrup and beaten egg . Mix until a firm dough forms.

Sprinkle a working area with flour and roll dough to a 12" x 14" rectangle. Using a round 2" cutter, cut out 32 biscuits. Place on a greased baking sheet and refrigerate at least one hour.

Bake at 350° for about 15 minutes or until dark brown. Remove from sheet onto a rack and sprinkle with a few tablespoons of sugar. Cool completely.

In a small bowl, cream butter with powdered sugar until creamy. In a double boiler, melt chocolate and add to the cream mixture. Beat until well blended. Add vanilla and continue beating until icing is easy to spread. Sandwich icing between two biscuits to form bonbons.

Makes 16 bonbons.

AMARETTO

AMARETTI

These classic pastries are traditionally served at Italian weddings and they are very easy to make. They can be kept crisp in a tightly covered container until the special day.

¹/₂	**pound almond paste**
1	**cup fine granulated sugar**
2	**egg whites**

Pre-heat oven to 325°. Cut almond paste into small pieces. Combine with sugar and egg whites. In a medium bowl, mix ingredients with hands, rubbing mixture between fingers until free of all lumps. Shape dough into 1" round cookies, keeping hands wet to keep dough from sticking. Place cookies on a greased baking sheet about 1" apart. Bake at 325° for 20 minutes.

Makes about 2 dozen.

ROSETTI FRITTI

ROSETTES

These crispy treats are classically Italian and made with a special iron found in any department store or specialty shop. The irons come in a variety of shapes and sizes, usually one rosette per iron, but sometimes two or more.

2	**eggs**
1	**teaspoon sugar**
1/4	**teaspoon salt**
1	**cup milk**
1	**cup flour, sifted**
4	**cups canola oil**

In a medium bowl, beat eggs with sugar and salt. Add milk and flour and beat until smooth. Batter should be thin.

Heat oil in deep fryer to 400°. Heat rosette iron in hot oil for 15 seconds then dip hot iron into the batter. Take care not to let batter come over top of iron. Lower iron into hot oil and fry rosettes 2–3 minutes until light brown. Lift iron from oil and gently pry rosettes off. If the rosette separates from the iron while frying, remove with a slotted spoon. Drain on paper towels. Repeat with remaining batter. Arrange rosettes on serving tray and dust with powdered sugar.

Makes 40 rosettes.

PIZZELLE
WAFER COOKIES

To make these pastries you need a pizzele iron, which is similar to a waffle iron except it creates rounded, flat cookies with an attractive lacy design. They can be found in department stores or speciality stores and the investment will really pay off when your family and friends taste the results.

12	eggs
3	cups sugar
2	cups canola oil
3/4	cup anisette liqueur
4	tablespoons anise seeds
4	cups flour
4	tablespoons baking powder
1/4	teaspoon salt

Heat pizzele iron to recommended temperature. In a large mixing bowl, beat eggs, sugar and oil. Add liqueur, anise seeds, flour, baking powder and salt. If mixture becomes too thick, thin with water or juice. Pour small amount into hot pizzele iron and cook according to iron directions.

Makes approximately 4 dozen pizzelles.

Lexicon

Almond – Mandorla

Amaretti – Amaretto

Anise – Anisi

Apple – Pomo

Applesauce – Salsa di Mela

Apricot – Albicocca

Baking Powder – Lievito

Banana – Banana

Berry – Fragola

Birthday – Complianno

Biscuits – Panini

Bits – Pizzetti

Blueberry – Bacca Blu

Bonbons – Bombone

Brandy – Acquaviate, Acquavite

Bread – Pani

Brownies – Pasticcini Abruenire

Buns – Muffulettini, Pannetti

Butter – Burro

Butterscotch – Caramella al Burro

Cake – Torta

Caramel – Caramelli

Carrot – Carota

Cereal – Cereale

Cheese – Formaggio, Ricotta, Cacio

Chocolate – Chocolati

Chocolate Chip – Pizzetti di
  Chocolati

Cinnamon – Cannella

Cocoa – Cacao

Coconut – Noce di Cocco

Coffee – Caffe

Cookies – Pasticcini, Biscotti,
  Biscottini

Corn – Grano

Cornflakes – Cereale di Grano

Cranberry – Mortella

Cream – Crema

Crescents – Pasticcini

Croissants – Panettini

Crust – Crosta

Custard – Crostata

Easter – Pasqua

Eclairs – Pasta Sfogliata

Fingers – Dito

Florentines – Fiorentine

Fresh – Fresca, Fresco

Fried – Fritto

Fritters – Sfingi

Fruit – Fruta

Ginger – Zenzero

Hazelnut – Nocciuolo

Holiday – Festa

Honey – Miele

Index – Indice

Large – Grandi

Lemon – Limone

Macaroons – Amaretti

Madeleins – Saviardi

Mandarin – Mandarini

Marble – Marmarizzato

Marshmallow – Altea

Meringue – Meringa

Mincemeat – Carne Fritata

Mint – Menta

Mocha – Caffe

Morning – Matina

Muffins – Panino, Muffulettini

Nectar – Nettare

Neapolitan – Napolitani

Norwegian – Norvegese

Nut – Noce

Oatmeal – Farinata d'Avena

Orange – Arangi

Pastry – Pasta

Peach – Peschi

Peanut – Arachide

Pie – Torta, Tortella

Pfefferneuse – Peppata

Pineapple – D'Ananasso

Poppy Seed – Simenza Papavero

Potato – Patata

Prune – Prugna

Puffs – Bignoli

Pumpkin – Zucca

Raisin – Uva Passa

Ravioli – Ravioli

Recipe – Ricetta

Rice – Riso

Rolls – Cannoli, Rottoli, Rotondi

Rosettes – Rosetti

Rum – Rum, Rosolio

Sesame Seed – Simenza

Sour – Agro

Spice – Spezie

Sponge Roll – Gellitina

Strawberry – Fragola

Strudel – Pannetonne

Sugar – Zuccaro

Sweet – Dolce

Tart – Crostata

Turnovers – Cassatelli, Focacia

Velvet – Velluto

Walnut – Noce

White – Bianca

Wine – Vino

Zucchini – Zucchini

Index